Dream girl.

Tobey closed red-haired w~~o~~... ~~j~~... back of his eyelids.

He was having so many strange feelings right now. Upon first thought, the book seemed macabre, gruesome, and completely made up.

Witches, warlocks, and demons didn't really exist, right?

But on second thought, what was the harm in trying? If it didn't work, fine. But if it did...

He opened his eyes and let the book fall open by itself.

The spread it showed was a ritual for a specific demon—a female demon. Or at least, a demon that looked like a woman... a woman with green skin, red hair, twisting ram horns, and glowing yellow eyes.

There was a crude rendering of the demon. It was called the Nyx.

The name echoed in his brain.

The Nyx is the Daughter of Chaos.

He was suddenly very excited... and somehow exhausted at the same time.

He read the instructions for the ritual. It didn't involve anything too weird or malicious, like animal sacrifice—just black candles, a symbol marked on the floor in chalk, and a drop of the summoner's own blood.

I can do this, Tobey thought, as he slid the book back under his mattress and turned out the light.

As he lay in bed with his eyes closed but his thoughts racing, he planned what he was going to do.

Surely the Nyx could help him get revenge on his bullies.

Saccharin Valley High Books
#1 VAMPIRES IN PARADISE
#2 DEADLY DATING
#3 UNDER HER SPELL

Supernatural Stars
PIPER'S STORY
TOBEY'S STORY

Also Available by the Same Deranged Author:

Saccharin Valley Twits Books
#1 THE BABYSITTER
#2 THE WITCH
#3 THE FORTUNE TELLER
#4 THE VAMPIRES PART ONE: BLOOD MOON
#5 THE VAMPIRES PART TWO:
   THROUGH THE LOOKING GLASS
#6 THE BABYSITTER II
#7 THE VISITOR

Saccharin Valley Twits: Super Hideous Editions
#1 THE TWINS AND THEIR ROCK-STAR WITCH
   BABYSITTER
#2 STEVEN'S EVIL TWIN
#3 JESSICA THE WITCH

SACCHARIN VALLEY HIGH
Super(natural) Star

Tobey's Story

Written by Polly Esther Rayon

Created by Lara Pontiff

Not endorsed by or affiliated with Francine Pascal (RIP) in any way. Just my usual horror parody shenanigans... Inspired by the Sweet Valley High "Super Stars" series by "Kate William" except with a heavy dose of satire and some supernatural shenanigans... And my original characters, Piper Quintin, the witch, and Tobey North, the warlock.

*To my Sa,
who always shared my love/hate relationship
with Sweet Valley, and encouraged my writing*

*You want to run through the night
but you find yourself afraid of the dark
Well your sights are true,
but something won't let you hit the mark...*

—The Killer Whales, "Marlene"

Chapter 1

"I'm so excited about the dance next Friday," Jessica Wastefeld said as she maneuvered the Jeep she and her twin sister shared into the parking lot at Saccharin Valley High School one Monday morning.

"But it's on Friday the 13th," Elizabeth teased. "Aren't you worried something *bad* will happen?"

Elizabeth thought superstitions were silly, but Jessica took them seriously. This was one of the many differences in their personalities, despite them looking absolutely identical. Both twins were five foot six inches tall, with slim, athletic, tanned bodies, sun-streaked golden hair, and blue-green eyes, the same color as the nearby Pacific Ocean.

Jessica laughed as she checked her reflection in the rearview mirror before getting out of the car. She was the twin who cared more about her looks. Not that Elizabeth didn't take care with her appearance, but Jessica usually wore lots of makeup and the trendiest, most revealing clothes, while Elizabeth tended to keep her style conservative. "As long as we don't walk under any ladders or break any mirrors, it'll be fine," Jessica said, with a smile that showed her dimple.

"Do you have a date yet?" Elizabeth asked.

Jessica frowned. "No. I haven't found anyone good enough for me so far."

"Oh, is this one of the books where you *meet* a really cute guy and fall head over heels for him, instead of being in an established relationship?"

"Must be," Jessica shrugged.

"Well, you'd better be careful. You know sometimes when that happens, it ends in disaster," Elizabeth cautioned. This was true—like when Jessica threw herself at a college-age guy named Scott Dangles and got in over her head. In other books, she was already dating someone—like Ken Cashews, quarterback on the football team, or A. J. Organ, a military kid from Atlanta.

"That's what makes it exciting." Now Jessica realized, if she didn't have a date here at the beginning of the book, then she'd probably meet someone amazing within the next few chapters. That was the way things tended to go around here. She was giddy just thinking about it.

"Well, anyway, *I* have a hot date," Elizabeth said with a mischievous smile, and her twin sister made a face. While Jessica dated an endlessly revolving door of cute guys (who were in plentiful supply at SVHS), Elizabeth remained steady with her longtime boyfriend, Todd Wilson. Jessica thought Todd was dull and didn't see what her sister saw in him.

"Oh really? Who?" Jessica said innocently.

Elizabeth smacked her sister on the arm. "Todd, of course."

"Speaking of dates, did you know that *Tobey North* asked me to the dance? I had a hard time not laughing in his face. He barely says a word to anyone since he's been here, and suddenly he thinks he can date *the* Jessica Wastefeld? What a loser."

Elizabeth pursed her lips. Tobey was quiet, sure, but she didn't think he was as bad as Jessica said. He always sat in the back row during homeroom, either with his head bent over a book or with his arm curled around some secret drawing. He didn't seem to have any friends, but Elizabeth always tried to see the best in people. Any minute now she'd reach out to him to ask if there was trouble at home, if he needed a tutor, or to try to interview him for the school paper, the *Oracle*. Whenever there was someone new mentioned in one of these books, it was only a matter of time before Jessica schemed to get with them (or snubbed them, depending on their level of attractiveness), and/or Elizabeth took pity on them.

"He's not *that* bad," Elizabeth protested. "He's just shy, I bet. Anyway, why are we in the first scene of the book?" Elizabeth asked. "It says on the cover, *Tobey's Story*."

"We're the main characters of this series, duh," Jessica said. "And Tobey North is too *creepy* to warrant having a whole book devoted to him. Did you know he has a pet tarantula?"

"Where did you hear that?" Elizabeth asked as they joined the throng of students entering the Romanesque facade of Saccharin Valley High School.

"I heard it from Cara, who heard it from Caroline Pierced, who heard it from Randy Macon." Cara Dogwalker was a cheerleader and one of Jessica's many friends. Caroline was a gossipy redhead who wore prim and preppy clothes, and Randy was a computer whiz who wore the requisite eyewear for such a thing: horn-rimmed glasses.

Elizabeth rolled her eyes. Jessica's fondness for gossip was another difference between the twins. Elizabeth didn't like spreading gossip, although she *did* write the gossip column for the *Oracle*. It was good-natured, though, not malicious, so that made it OK.

The bell rang, and the twins went their separate ways.

*   *   *

Tobey North felt like an outcast at Saccharin Valley High. He was Caucasian, like 99% of the school (which was odd in a town that purported to be in Southern California, where you'd think they'd have a bigger Latino population, or Asians, or Pacific Islanders. But, according to the creator of the books I'm parodying, [may she rest in peace], "those were different times.")

SACCHARIN VALLEY HIGH

Despite blending in due to skin tone, Tobey stood out in many other ways. He was tall, but not in a well-built, handsome way like most of the boys in the junior class. More gangly and awkward, with hands and feet that were a little too large, a long neck, and a prominent Adam's apple. The other kids had been calling him "beanpole" and "scarecrow" since middle school.

He had a pale face with ruddy lips, blue eyes, and brown hair that fell over in a wave one eye when he ducked his head. He wore clothes that other kids made fun of—a retro style that no one thought was cool, because they were all stuck in the present, the early 1990s, with their bright colors, high-waisted jeans, and fancy sneakers. His way of dressing, coupled with his quiet nature, made him prone to bullying.

Tobey sat in homeroom hunched over a drawing. He was drawing a girl he liked—a girl who existed only in his dreams. She was a witch, but you couldn't tell from the drawing—she wasn't wearing a pointy hat or carrying a broom. (That was kid stuff.) It was a line drawing, so it didn't show her fiery emerald eyes or her unnaturally red hair. But it *did* show her mysterious smile.

She was holding one hand up triumphantly—in the hand was a bleeding, anatomically correct disembodied heart, dripping down the page. It was *his* heart that the witch was holding, but she hadn't stolen it; it had been freely given.

He reached for a red pen to ink in the organ and its gushing blood.

"What's this, your girlfriend?" Charlie Cashbox, who was known for being a bully, had snatched the paper off his desk and was peering at it.

"Give it back," Tobey said in a low voice. He didn't like to talk much—it gave him a headache for some reason. His words came out in an American accent, like all the other students, even though his mom was British. Tobey's dad had walked out on them when he was five. As a kid, Tobey had always tried to talk "normal" in school so the other kids wouldn't make fun of him—and the American accent had gradually taken over. It was only lately that it felt weird to talk this way.

Tobey's Story

"Gross, what is this chick holding?" Charlie said disgustedly as his eyes traveled down the page. He crumpled the paper and threw it to the floor. "You're a freak, North."

Tobey's chest tightened, but he didn't say anything. He waited until Charlie had sauntered off, then got up to grab the crumpled paper ball off the floor, tenderly smoothing it out.

The girl in the drawing didn't exist, but that didn't mean he would stop drawing her.

Someday he'd find her—and then all the bullies would be sorry.

He looked up and saw that Elizabeth Wastefeld was smiling at him sympathetically. He forced himself to smile back. He knew he should be thrilled that one of the pretty, popular Wastefeld twins was acknowledging his existence—but he wasn't impressed.

In fact, he was kind of annoyed.

If she's really such a do-gooder, she'd be able to do something about this bullying, he thought.

The bell rang, and he walked out the door. Elizabeth Wastefeld was calling out to him, asking him something, but he pretended he hadn't heard and kept going.

That afternoon, Jessica honked the horn at her sister, who was chatting with her best friend, Enid Maudlin, as they left the school building for the day.

"What gives?" Elizabeth said as she reached the car. "Are you that eager to start on your homework?" Her blue-green eyes sparkled, as they were wont to do, at least once per book.

Jessica rolled her eyes. "Of course not. I just need to go shopping for a dress for the dance, so the sooner we get home, the better." Seeing Elizabeth casually throw her backpack in the back seat, she added, "Come *on*, Liz. I don't have all day."

"OK, OK," Elizabeth muttered as she fastened her seatbelt. At least her sister was giving her a ride, instead of leaving her stranded. Jessica started the car, and the engine roared to life. She peeled out of the parking lot, going ten miles over the speed limit.

"Why are you in such a hurry?" Elizabeth asked, holding onto the side door as Jessica careened around a corner. "The dance isn't until next Friday."

"I know!" Jessica declared, purposefully misconstruing her sister's remark. "If I don't find something this afternoon, I'm doomed!" Jessica was always inclined to be overdramatic. Elizabeth was probably going to wear something from her own closet—something she'd worn *on a previous occasion*. Her twin wouldn't be caught dead wearing the same outfit to a different dance.

She pulled into the driveway of the Wastefeld's split-level ranch house on Calicorny Drive. They'd made the trip in record time. Elizabeth was barely out of the car before Jessica threw it into reverse and waved. "See you later!"

Elizabeth just smiled and shook her head, going up the front walk. Jessica was something else. (This didn't frustrate her; it charmed her. What a weirdo.)

Once Jessica got downtown, she headed for her favorite store, Giselle's. But as she got to the end of the freeway exit, she saw a new store in a shopping center just up ahead. Excitedly, she made a turn without signaling.

It was a trendy boutique called Seraphina's, and inside the front window display was the perfect dress. Jessica pulled into a parking spot and dashed inside.

Every dress in the store was exactly her size—a perfect size six.

Tobey staggered down the steps of the school. It was the end of the day, finally, and he was sore from being shoved in a locker.

He'd also been mercilessly teased in gym class, and in Pre-Calculus, he had caught a classmate of his, Ronnie Upwards, using his test paper to cheat. Then *he'd* gotten in trouble with the teacher.

Tobey's Story

This is just not right, he thought, as he got into his beat-up Toyota. *How is this my life?*

Two miles from home, he got a flat tire.

    *   *   *

"Lila, I just *have* to tell you about this new store I found," Jessica said into the phone later that evening. Lila Fouler, Jessica's best friend, was the only daughter of one of the wealthiest men in Saccharin Valley and wanted for nothing.

"What store? If it's worth shopping at, I probably already know it," Lila said in a bored tone.

"No, it just popped up," Jessica insisted. "And I found the most perfect dress!"

"OK, I'll bite," Lila said. "Where is this amazing store?"

Jessica told her the address.

"I'll check it out on the way home from school tomorrow," Lila said. "Just to satisfy my curiosity."

"You're late," Mrs. North said in a no-nonsense tone when Tobey got home. He'd had a spare tire, but somehow had misplaced his jack, so he'd had to walk to find a phone, call a tow truck, and have his car towed to the nearest auto shop. By the time the tire had been fixed, it was already dark and he was exhausted. "You should've had dinner ready hours ago. I'm counting on you, Tobias. I know it's hard, but we just have to make the best of it." Mrs. North worked a full-time job as a clerk in a high-end boutique and also part-time as a horticulturist in an exotic plant nursery.

"Sorry, Mother," he said glumly. "I had some trouble with my car. Can I fix you a cup of tea and make us some sandwiches?"

"That would be lovely," Mrs. North said.

Tobey prepared the tea the way she liked it, with a squeeze of fresh lemon—they had a tree in their backyard—and a dollop of local wildflower honey.

Then he started rooting through the refrigerator. He found the bread, and the sliced deli meat he'd gotten the day before. In a few minutes, he had two delicious sandwiches, each artfully arranged on a plate with apple slices and a pickle.

"Mother, can I ask you about... Dad?" Tobey said after he'd taken his first bite.

His mother paused just as she was about to pick up her sandwich. She sighed. There was sadness in her pale violet-blue eyes. "Not now, Tobias, dear. I'm very tired."

He knew not to push the issue, so they finished the meal in silence.

Later, he couldn't focus on his homework. All he could think about was his father. It was odd, since he had very few memories of him. Mr. North had left when Tobey was very young, and his mother had always told him he was a bad guy, so he'd always just left it at that.

But this morning when he'd dreamed about the red-haired witch, it was different than usual. She was in his house, pointing at the attic door. She seemed to be trying to tell him something, something important, but he couldn't make out the words.

So after his mother was asleep, he crept up to the attic.

The attic was accessible only by a narrow, rickety staircase in the back of the house. He knew which step creaked, and skipped over it so it wouldn't make noise. He opened the door as quietly as he could, slipped inside, and turned on the light. The light was pretty dim, but it was enough to see by.

He knew exactly what he was looking for.

There was a beat-up black steamer trunk in the back of the attic. All his life it had been locked—but there had been a steady drip from the ceiling for the last year and now the lock had rusted and corroded. It crumbled under his hands. He opened the lid.

Inside, there were some clothes of his father's, some tools, and a book.

But the clothes weren't ordinary clothes. They looked like a fantastical costume—one that a medieval sorcerer would wear. There was a dark blue robe with a cowl and a hood and silver trim, and a pair of scuffed black boots with what looked like dried blood on the toes.

After examining these, he looked at the tools, which didn't belong on a workbench. There were black candles, pale-green chalk, a silver dagger, and a small cauldron that went on a stand. There was also a brass incense censer.

He picked up each tool, one by one, turning them over in his hands. His heart was beating furiously. What was all this stuff?

Finally, he pulled out a black mirror, and before he could see his own reflection, he thought he could make out the reflection of a redheaded woman, just for an instant. She was smiling.

This must've been what she wanted to tell me, he thought excitedly as the woman vanished from the mirror. *That my father had some sort of secret life...*

He picked up the book. It was filled with small, cramped script and strange diagrams. He couldn't make heads or tails of it.

But inside the front cover was an address penciled in on the top corner—it was a shop in downtown Saccharin Valley.

The Book Cellar, it said. He liked the play on words—"cellar" instead of "seller." Was this bookstore really in a basement? Those weren't common in California...

Tobey gathered the candles, the dagger, and the book and put them in a small, empty cardboard box that was sitting on top of a pile of junk.

Then he turned out the light and stealthily made his way back downstairs to his room.

*   *   *

That night, Tobey didn't see the red-headed witch in his dreams. Instead, he was an evil sorcerer, in black robes. He was wearing a skullcap over his hair, and he had a pointed goatee. He was preparing an altar on the cold stone floor of a crumbling castle tower.

SACCHARIN VALLEY HIGH

Inside a pentacle drawn on the floor in blood, Elizabeth Wastefeld was chained to her homeroom desk, looking terrified. "I just wanted to help you!" she sobbed.

"And so you are, my dear, just not in the way you think," he said in a velvet voice, his eyes shining. He chuckled, and there was nothing nervous or awkward about it... only delicious sinister intent. "You are perfect for sacrificing on my altar, as this demon I am summoning prefers the blood of *virgins*."

Elizabeth gasped, turned bright red, and smacked him across the face, her chains rattling as she did so. "How dare you! Virginity is a social construct, *and* it refers to the dark days when men treated women like property, linking their worth to their supposed purity—"

"It's the 90s, they *still* do that," he interjected.

Elizabeth shook her head. "No, I'm a *liberated* woman," she insisted. "I *chose* to be Todd's girlfriend... and occasionally his mother/nursemaid. Besides, we never outright *say* 'virgin' in these books. We just *allude* to it. I'm *good,* so I don't have sex, the reader assumes, but Jessica's a party girl. However, this doesn't make her a slut, like 'Easy Annie'. Jessica's wild and *bad,* but she's still somehow as virginal as I am! It's a paradox, really."

Tobey stared at her. His victim was a little too self-aware. Maybe he should've grabbed Jessica instead. *Jessica* would've just screamed and sobbed, like she was supposed to.

"Yes, that is very messed up, but also a product of its time," Evil Sorcerer Tobey said hurriedly as he sharpened his silver dagger. Elizabeth watched the gleaming blade fearfully. The moon had risen, and it was time. He gave her a wicked smile as he raised the dagger over his head. "Now hold still."

Elizabeth screamed, long and loud.

The next morning, well, there are certain things, certain *specific* aspects of puberty, that are never mentioned in these types of books, but suffice to say, it had been a *good* dream for Tobey.

He pulled his sheets off the bed to load the washer before his mom got up.

Chapter 2

Elizabeth Wastefeld awoke from a very strange dream. It was about Tobey North, the shy, gangly boy in her homeroom class.

In the dream, he was sexy, utterly confident—and an *evil sorcerer*. He was going to drain her blood to sacrifice her on an altar!

She blushed just thinking about it.

What a silly dream, she thought. *I must've eaten something spicy too close to bedtime.*

She decided that in this one instance, it would be allowable *not* to meddle in the life of—I mean, *offer help to*—a student who was struggling.

Sure, Tobey was being bullied, but so were a lot of kids. Bullying was rife at Saccharin Valley High School (usually when integral to the plot). She didn't need to get involved *every* time.

She breathed a sigh of relief when she got to homeroom and saw that Tobey's usual seat in the back was empty. Normally, he acted as if the other students weren't there, so it wasn't as if he'd approach *her,* anyway.

She left homeroom to check in at the *Oracle* office before school.

SACCHARIN VALLEY HIGH

*   *   *

Tobey got to school late, missing homeroom, but it didn't matter, because he felt fantastic. He'd worn an outfit more like the other boys wore—jeans and a T-shirt, but with his black Doc Martens instead of fancy sneakers. Nobody took any notice of this change of outfit, which was good. As long as he remained invisible and didn't get into trouble, he could visit the bookstore after school.

He managed to get through the day without running into either of the Wastefeld twins, which was a relief, since they seemed to be everywhere all the time. The entire student body *adored* them.

He couldn't deal with Elizabeth's pity or Jessica's revulsion currently.

But... he had a feeling they'd soon get what was coming to them.

His morning classes went without incident, and he ate lunch alone, as was his preference. Even the geeks —as Jessica called them—didn't dare sit with him.

Besides, he'd cooked his lunch himself, as opposed to partaking in the depressing, boiled-into-oblivion cafeteria options. He'd brought minestrone in a thermos and in a bento box, a panzanella salad, sliced fruit, and for dessert, panna cotta.

After fruit and before dessert, he felt like someone was watching him. He glanced up and saw Tom McLay—a good-looking boy with a *secret*—staring at him. Once Tom saw him looking, he looked away in embarrassment.

Tobey suddenly realized what else was wrong with this school, besides it being too *white*. It was also so... what was the word?

Heteronormative.

In the hallways of Saccharin Valley High, minutes before the bell rang for his next class, Tobey navigated through the crowd of students and made his way to his locker.

Tobey's Story

There was a strange croaking noise coming from inside. He spun the combination and opened it—and dozens of live frogs jumped out.

The students at the lockers around him jumped and shrieked as the frogs frantically hopped away from their temporary prison. Some kids tried to catch them, and some kids—girls mostly—screamed when a frog jumped past them.

The chemistry teacher came out to see what all the fuss was about and called the janitor to come help him round up the frogs.

At the end of the hallway, Charlie Cashbox was watching Tobey with a satisfied smirk on his face.

In her last class of the day, Health, Elizabeth sank into a chair next to her boyfriend, Todd. She sighed.

"What's eating you?" Todd wanted to know.

"It's Tobey North," Elizabeth said. "I wasn't going to meddle, but he just keeps being bullied..."

"Oh, yeah, those frogs were hilarious. I don't think they got them all, either. I still hear croaking in the halls..."

"Todd, it's not funny. I really wish they would stop," Elizabeth said.

Todd just grunted.

"Can't you do something about it?" Elizabeth went on in a coaxing tone.

"Me?" squawked Todd. "*I'm* not bothering Tobey..."

"No, but Charlie is, and some other boys. Can't you talk to them?"

"Liz, it's nice of you to be concerned, but I don't think *me* talking to the bullies will do anything," Todd said. "It might even make me a target."

"Well, at least they'd actually listen to you," Elizabeth hedged.

"What, just because I'm a *guy*?" Todd argued. "Aren't you into women's lib and all that stuff? Who says a girl can't go tell off a guy's bullies?"

SACCHARIN VALLEY HIGH

"I don't want to make Tobey feel worse," Elizabeth said. "Knowing a girl was sticking up for him, ..."

"It seems like you already know the answer to this problem," Todd said. "Just let it go."

Elizabeth frowned, and the bell rang. She opened up her textbook, which was conveniently missing the chapter on STDs, and probably preached abstinence.

She remembered her dream and shivered.

As *good* a girl as she was... she had kind of *liked* it.

*   *   *

Tobey pulled into the parking lot of the address he'd written down. He didn't see any signs for a bookstore.

Straight ahead was a trendy boutique, and as he walked up to it, he saw a sign on the side of the building. It said *The Book Cellar* and had an arrow pointing down a set of concrete steps in the alleyway.

He went down the steps and pushed open the door at the bottom. The door creaked on its hinges. It was dimly lit inside—more of a dank basement room than a store. There was a musty old book smell with an overtone of incense.

There were bookshelves lining the concrete walls floor to ceiling, stuffed with books. But these were no ordinary books—they all had something to do with the occult—spells, curses, demonology, unexplained phenomena, psychic abilities. There were even books about supernatural creatures like vampires and werewolves. All the books were used; some were old and crumbling hardbacks while others were merely dusty and faded paperbacks.

In the back was a slight man with longish brown hair graying at the temples and shining dark brown eyes. He was wearing a faded flannel shirt and examining some kind of amulet, half-covered in crusted filth, under a large magnifying glass on a movable arm. Behind him was a locked glass case filled with rare and sinister-looking volumes.

Tobey's Story

He looked up as Tobey approached. "Can I help you?" He had a Scottish accent.

"I'm—just looking," Tobey stammered.

The man regarded him with shrewd eyes. "We don't get a lot of browsers down here," he said. "Was there something in particular you're looking *for*?"

Tobey glanced around helplessly at all the moldering tomes. "Well, I'm looking for something—something—" he shut his eyes briefly, wincing—"something to help me with being bullied at school," he finished, letting out his breath all at once. He couldn't believe he'd just said that. It was beyond humiliating.

The man stared at him. "Usually, folks do not come into an occult store for assistance with that particular problem... have you tried telling a trusted adult?" His slight smile was almost a smirk.

Tobey looked miserable. "I don't know any," he muttered. He looked at the strange jewelry item on the counter. "Erm, how does one get into the occult, exactly?"

"You don't. The occult gets into you," the man informed him. "I'm Mr. August, by the way."

"Tobey," Tobey said. He shook the man's hand.

Mr. August turned his attention back to his work. Tobey thought this was unusual. Wasn't he interested in selling books? He couldn't make sales by ignoring customers...

His heart started beating a little faster as he thought about what to say next. *Here goes nothing.* "As to that—the occult—well, I've been having a peculiar recurring dream lately..."

"A dream, you say?" Mr. August grunted, not looking up. "Dream dictionaries are on Aisle Four." He continued examining the item under the magnifying glass.

"No, it's not that—I don't need help *interpreting* the dream," Tobey said quickly. "It's about a girl. A woman, I mean. She seems like someone I've met before... but I don't know anyone like her at school..."

"Could be you met her in a past life," Mr. August said, prodding the amulet with a tool of some kind. Some encrusted dirt flaked off. "Or she could be a succubus..."

Here he stopped and looked up. His dark eyes were shining. "What does the dream *feel* like?"

"Good," Tobey said, his face flushing in embarrassment.

"Say no more, laddie," Mr. August said with a knowing look. "But what does this have to do with bullying?"

"Well, uh, it kind of seems like she can help me?" Tobey, wondering how much more he could say about his dream before the man decided to kick him out for pulling his leg.

"What does she look like?"

"Why does that matter?" Tobey hedged.

"Well, if she says she can help you, that could refer to any number of entities," Mr. August explained, turning the light off his magnifier and pushing it out of the way. The piece he'd been examining got locked in a drawer under the cash register. "Fae, merfolk, nymphs... or something with more devious intent, like a demon or a djinn... if you tell me what she looks like, it might help narrow it down."

"Oh," Tobey said. Somehow telling a man he'd just met what his dream girl looked like seemed very personal. At the same time, he was in pretty deep already. It would be pointless to stop now. "She has very red hair, more crimson than natural red. And eyes like emeralds... she's also pretty tall, about my height."

"Hmm, doesn't ring a bell," Mr. August mused. He came out from behind the counter, running his hand along the spines of the books shelved at eye level, until he found the one he was looking for. "Aha!" He pulled the book out and handed it to Tobey. "Try this."

It was a slim volume with a worn cloth cover. It looked more like someone's old journal than a book on the occult. It said *Witchcraft*—or maybe *Witchcrafte*—on the side, in letters that were almost rubbed off completely. Tobey started to open it, but Mr. August put his hands over the cover. "Not here," he said. "Wait until you get home."

Tobey gave him a puzzled look. Why would he buy a book without looking inside first?

Tobey's Story

At the same time, the book felt kind of... warm, as if it were alive. He could see the witch from his dream in his mind. Her green eyes were glowing, and she was grinning and nodding.

"How much?"

"That'll be nine ninety-nine," Mr. August said.

Tobey paid with crumpled bills from his pocket. As he headed for the door, Mr. August said, "Let me know how it goes."

*   *   *

Lila pulled her lime-green Triumph into the parking lot of the address Jessica had given her. She couldn't read her own writing—it either said Suite *B* or Suite *D*. She looked up and realized that Suite B was a vacant storefront up for lease. She walked down to Suite D, her Italian leather heels clacking on the pavement, and frowned. Hadn't Jessica said the name of the store was Seraphina's? This store said ROWAN and seemed to be an upscale boutique.

That was more up her alley, anyway. After all, she was rich; she didn't need to shop in the bargain basement.

She pushed open the door.

There were dresses in the window display, but in here she could only see some fancy chairs and a podium, and beyond that, the rest of the store was separated by a brocade curtain.

"Do you have an appointment?" The woman behind the podium was almost six feet tall, slim, with blonde hair cut in a short, chic style and unnaturally large ice-blue eyes. She was wearing an exquisitely tailored grey suit with a silk scarf and a jeweled brooch shaped like a sprig of blackthorn.

"No, I don't, but my gold card does," Lila said with a dazzling smile, flashing her credit card.

The woman glanced at the card and nodded. "Very well, Ms. Fouler. My staff and I will be *happy* to serve you."

*   *   *

When he got home, Tobey hid the *Witchcraft* book under his mattress. The other book, his father's book that he couldn't read, was in the box with the other things, buried in the bottom of his closet. There was no time to look at the new book now—there were chores to be done, homework to finish, and he had to make dinner for his mom, who always worked late on weekdays.

When he was finally able to open the book, it was an hour past his usual bedtime. He crawled into bed and switched his bedside lamp on, then retrieved the book from its hiding place.

He'd expected it to be a general guide to witchcraft, or perhaps a history, but instead, the few first pages were superstitions and folklore about witches.

"It was once said that a woman with red hair was a witch."

Check, Tobey thought. The woman in his dream was a witch, and she had red hair.

"Sometimes a woman with a birthmark would be accused of witchcraft. Or if she had an extra finger."

Tobey skimmed this paragraph, as he knew his witch did not have either of those features. She had a mole under her right eye, but that was hardly a witch's mark. Tobey read on.

"Male witches exist, but they are rare. There are also other names for specific types of male magic users. One such name is **Warlock***"*—

Tobey's stomach lurched. At first the word "Warlock" looked like it was in bold type, but then he blinked and it was regular again.

Warlock.

The word gave him a funny feeling... a *familiar* feeling.

"Male magic users can also be consorts to witches. They derive their power solely through one specific witch, and the witch controls what magical deeds the consort can perform.

In exchange for this borrowed power, the male is granted permission to lie with the witch on her holy days, the sabbats and esbats; and this replenishes her aura and strengthens her power."

Tobey's Story

This sounded familiar too. Although, being a teenager in an early-1990s YA novel, the phrase "lie with" made him blush, probably. (Geeks in these books are never secure in their sexuality.)

He read on.

"A warlock does not have the same level of power as a witch, but can summon demons, usually through a ritual involving lighting candles, marking the floor or ground with a special sign, and drawing blood, as an offering."

His left palm began to tingle.

"Once the demon is summoned, it is bound to the magic circle until given license to depart. The demon can give the warlock more power, but at a price."

Tobey closed the book and shut his eyes tightly. The red-haired woman from his dreams appeared on the back of his eyelids.

He was having so many strange feelings right now. Upon first thought, the book seemed macabre, gruesome, and definitely fictional.

Witches, warlocks, and demons didn't really exist, right?

But on second thought, what was the harm in trying? If it didn't work, fine. But if it did...

He opened his eyes and let the book fall open by itself.

He could see that some pages had been ripped out where the book had opened. What was missing, he wondered?

Right after the missing pages was a ritual for a specific demon—a *female* demon. Or at least, a demon that looked like a woman... a woman with moss-green skin, red hair, twisting ram horns, and glowing yellow eyes.

There was a crude rendering of the demon, almost like a woodcut. It was called the Nyx.

The name echoed in his brain.

"The Nyx is the Daughter of Chaos."

He was suddenly very excited... and exhausted at the same time.

He read the instructions for the ritual. It didn't involve anything too weird or malicious. He would need a drop of his own blood.

I can do this, Tobey thought, as he slid the book back under his mattress and turned out the light.

As he lay in bed with his eyes closed but his thoughts racing, he planned what he was going to do.

Surely the Nyx could help him get revenge on his bullies.

Chapter 3

Lila called Jessica once she got home, while a servant brought in her stack of parcels from Rowan. It had been a wildly successful shopping trip. The glamorous store owner had been to London, Paris, Rome, and Athens. *A*nd *s*he was personally acquainted with a few of Lila's favorite designers.

"What gives?" she said when Jessica answered. "That store you were talking about wasn't there."

"What?" Jessica said. "Of course it is. I have the receipt for my dress right here—I used my mom's credit card, of course, and if I get in trouble I'll just blame Liz... Are you sure you had the right address?"

"Yes," Lila said immediately, not mentioning the part about her illegible handwriting. The point was moot, though, because of the vacant building she'd seen. "It was an empty storefront, with a sign saying 'For Lease'. Anyway, in the same shopping center, I found the most exclusive boutique, so it wasn't a wasted trip."

She kicked off her shoes and sank into a chair, eyeing the pile of parcels appreciatively. The glossy dress boxes were covered in a design of stark, thorny branches.

"What boutique?" Jessica asked. "All I saw, besides Seraphina's, was a dry cleaner and a pet groomer."

"It was called Rowan," Lila said happily. "They only sell designer originals."

"Are you sure *that* wasn't Seraphina's?" Jessica asked in confusion.

"Of course I'm sure," Lila snapped. "It said 'Rowan' on the sign, it was a *completely* different store, and *you* wouldn't have been able to afford any of it."

Jessica grumbled over the phone. Lila was her best friend, but never missed an opportunity to flaunt her riches.

"Well, maybe I'll go again after school tomorrow and see what's going on," Jessica mused. "I was *just there*. It would be a shame if *your* hoity-toity exclusive store forced *my* independently owned little funky boutique out of the shopping center with its high prices."

"You can't go tomorrow," Lila said. "We have cheerleading practice."

"Fine," Jessica sighed, then hung up.

For the first time in several weeks, Tobey awoke from a night without dreams. It had been restful, but where had the glamorous dream witch gone? He'd been looking forward to asking her about the Nyx demon. Even though he'd only seen her in dreams, she seemed *real*.

Most of the time when he dreamed of her, she didn't speak. He'd asked her name over and over, to no avail. Whenever he did, she just smiled sadly. That was what had made the new dream about her, when she showed him the attic door, so exciting.

Maybe tonight I'll see her. In the meantime, he would focus on gathering supplies. He just *knew* that summoning the Nyx demon was his ticket out of here.

At school the next day, everyone was chattering excitedly about the dance. The dance committee had decided to use lucky charms for decor, since the date had fallen on Friday the 13th. They'd scatter the tables with bright shiny pennies, nail horseshoes over the doorways, and hand out lucky rabbit's feet. Someone on the

Tobey's Story

committee had been given the dubious task of trying to find potted four-leaf clovers. The punch would have exactly seven ingredients, and the attendees would be encouraged to wear their favorite colors and any 'lucky' jewelry they owned.

The bullies, unfortunately, did not let up just because they were focused on getting dates to the dance. They were very good at multitasking. Tobey narrowly avoided getting his head dunked in a toilet, was purposely tripped multiple times in the hall, and several people muttered "Freak" as he walked by, or even croaked like frogs, referring to yesterday's events.

But he didn't care. He had a secret to keep him going. That Friday, he'd be performing the summoning ritual. It was the new moon, and the book had said the ritual was best performed under "darkness of moon."

He'd made it through the gauntlet of bullying to his locker, which someone had spray-painted a badly rendered pentagram on. Tobey took a deep breath and reminded himself it was almost the end of the day. He just had to hold out for one more class.

The locker still smelled like frog juice, and when he opened it, a piece of paper fell out. Olivia Jaded-One, a funky artist (whose visage, interestingly, went from seemingly Black or mixed race to straight-up mayonnaise person in the span of a few book covers) was walking by just then, and she stopped to pick it up. "Oh, you dropped this."

She glanced at it before handing it back to him. Tobey could see it was one of his dream witch drawings. The witch was holding one hand palm up, kindling a magic flame, which he'd inked with highlighters to make it look like it was glowing. He held his breath, wondering what she'd say.

"Wow, this is really good," she said, her hazel eyes wide.

Of course it's good, he wanted to say. *I'm merely a conduit for this witch's power.*

"T-thanks," he managed to stammer. He could feel the headache from talking coming on.

"I mean, really," Olivia said. "Your line work is exquisite. And I love that the only use of color in the red in her hair, and the green of the flame... red and green are complementary colors, but you must know that."

Tobey snatched the drawing and stuffed it back in his locker. He couldn't think what else to say. In another world, the world of his dreams, he was smooth and suave and could charm anybody, especially pretty girls.

But here in the waking world, he felt like a toad.

And not even a nice toad that a witch would keep as a pet.

"You're Tobey, aren't you?" Olivia said.

"Y-yes," he said, stuttering again. "Tobey North."

"Do you take any art classes? You'd love them," she went on.

"No, not at present," Tobey said. "I don't have much time for after-school activities."

"Or you could join the art club," Olivia said. "It meets twice a month."

Tobey knew that wasn't possible, given all that he had to do at home. Most kids at Saccharin Valley High School had two parents. Even the kids whose parents were divorced usually had a step-parent. As such, they could participate in any extracurriculars they wanted. It wasn't fair.

He looked up and saw that Olivia was looking at him, about to say something. Suddenly Tobey *knew* she was going to ask him to the dance. He could tell her he had a girlfriend, who went to another school. Olivia was nice, and pretty, but Tobey only had eyes for the dream witch.

She opened her mouth to speak, but the bell rang. Tobey shot down the hallway without looking back.

That night, Tobey consulted the book one last time to make sure he had everything he needed. It was getting closer to the new moon, and he wanted to be sure everything was perfect. It would be agony to have to wait twenty-eight more days if something went wrong.

There were five black candles, one for each point of the pentacle. The five-pointed star would be drawn inside two circles, one inside the other. In the space between the circles, and in between the points of the star, he would draw five magical symbols. He was surprised to see that one of them was his own astrological symbol, Aquarius. Was that symbol supposed to be customized to the user, or did the book somehow know his sign? And then he noticed another astrological sign among the five symbols: Sagittarius. He tried to think if he knew anybody who was a Sagittarius... but he wasn't close enough to anybody to talk about something so personal. It was mostly airheaded girls at school who talked about astrology, anyway. (He knew the Wastefeld twins were Geminis, which was a little on the nose.)

There was another symbol in the very center of the pentacle, but it had a small stain obscuring part of it. He scraped at it delicately with his fingernail. It kind of looked like the symbol for Aries.

Why was there a third astrological sign on the diagram? Who did it represent? Or what?

Then he remembered the rendering of the Nyx. He flipped back a page to look. Aries was the ram, and the Nyx had ram horns.

So maybe it wasn't an astrological sign, but a symbol for the demon. Interesting.

Once he had the magical diagram memorized, he took out the silver dagger and tested its sharpness. He'd use the dagger to draw blood, let it drip in the center of the pentacle, and then speak the summoning incantation, which seemed to be in Latin. He'd need to make sure he could pronounce all of it correctly.

He frowned at the words. He might need to get help with pronunciation. Other than that, he was set.

The excitement flared up in his stomach like the green flame he'd drawn being kindled in the witch's clawed hand.

That night, he dreamed about her again, but this dream was different. Instead of them being together, as if they'd known each other for a long time, soulmates, lovers... he was trying to catch up to her as she was running away.

"Stop!" he cried. "Wait! I just want to talk to you!"

His dream-lungs felt like they were going to burst. He pumped his dream-legs harder, but the witch was swift, practically flying.

He heard her voice come on the wind: *I'm sorry.*

"Just tell me your name!" he pleaded.

Piper, the wind moaned.

He sat up in bed, sweating. It was great that he knew her name now, but he'd wanted to ask about the Nyx.

And if he was her witch's consort, or a warlock. (If anybody knew this, it'd be his dream witch, since his father was unavailable for questioning.)

I guess I'll find out, he thought, getting dressed for school.

During his study period, he managed to track down the Latin teacher that some of the Advanced-Placement seniors took classes from, Mr. Cato. Mr. Cato was a short man with a bald head.

"I-I was wondering if you could help me," he said. He showed the teacher the passage in the *Witchcraft* book, grateful that the title on the spine was mostly rubbed off. (Also, the woodcut of the Nyx was on the previous page, so Mr. Cato wouldn't see that.)

"What's this about?" Mr. Cato asked, putting on a pair of reading glasses.

"It's for extra credit... in my Spanish class," Tobey invented. "The assignment was to translate something from a different language into English, and then into Spanish."

"Oh," Mr. Cato said, blinking. He studied the print on the page, frowning. "Well, this seems to be in the imperative tense... you know, a command. '*Prodire*' means '*come forth*'... hmm." He looked over the words again. "Are you sure *this* is the passage you want to use? It seems like some sort of ancient... *spell.*" Mr. Cato's eyes twinkled. He clearly didn't believe in such things, but seemed curious about the passage.

Tobey's Story

"Well, uh, we're learning about the Inquisition in History class..." Tobey was starting to think showing this particular book to a teacher was a bad idea. But he wanted to make sure he got the summoning right. "I really just needed help with the pronunciation."

"Oh, I see," said Mr. Cato. "That I can do. As a general rule, Cs and Gs are always hard, and 'v' sounds like a 'w'... here, let me jot some things down for you." He pulled a scratch pad out of a desk drawer and scribbled some things on it. "I'm adding some notes about syllabic emphasis, too. There." He finished writing and pulled the page crisply off the pad. "Now, I've got some papers to grade, if you don't mind."

"Thank you," Tobey said, taking the paper. Then he hurried from the classroom.

That's done, he thought in relief, striding down the hall. *Now I just have to get through today and tomorrow.*

He nearly collided with Elizabeth Wastefeld on his way back to his own classroom. In true rom-com fashion, she'd been holding a stack of papers, and they went in all directions as she lost her balance and fell forward.

To Tobey's surprise, he swiftly caught her. Usually his reflexes weren't this good. "Sorry about that," he said, letting go of her as soon as she was back on her feet. He knelt down to start picking up the papers.

"No, it was my fault," Elizabeth said, sounding a little out of breath.

She helped him gather the papers up, and he handed them to her in a messy stack. One page had fallen several feet away from her, and when she walked over and picked it up, she frowned. "Oh, this isn't mine," she said. She held it out to him.

Tobey's stomach plummeted when he saw. How did one of his drawings get in Elizabeth's stack of papers? This one wasn't of the red-headed witch, but he recognized the style immediately as his own. It showed two twin girls, gorgeous, busty teenagers, dressed head to toe in Medieval armor. Only their heads were showing, and that was how he could tell they were twins. The heart-shaped faces were identical, but the one on the left had her hair pulled back in barrettes, and the one on the right had her hair down around her shoulders in loose waves. He'd inked the latter girl's lips in blood red, and both pairs of eyes were colored aquamarine, with tiny dots of white-out to make them look sparkling.

I don't remember drawing this, he thought, his stomach knotting. But it was definitely his drawing. His initials were scribbled in the bottom corner: THORN. He snatched the paper out of Elizabeth's hands and hastily folded it up, shoving it into his pocket. He could feel his ears turning red with embarrassment.

"Oh, um, that was a really nice drawing," Elizabeth offered, with a tentative smile. "It kind of looked like..."

He didn't let her finish, just ran in the other direction.

Tom McLay was sitting in the back of the study hall classroom, and looked up when Tobey came in. He was scowling.

*   *   *

Elizabeth stayed after school to work on the *Oracle,* so she told Jessica she'd get a ride home with Enid. Mr. Collins was in the *Oracle* office, and Olivia was there too, as she sometimes drew cartoons for the paper.

"Elizabeth," she said hesitantly, "Uh... is Tobey North in your homeroom?"

"Yes, why?"

"I just wanted to ask him something," Olivia said. "I don't think he has any afterschool activities, so he must go straight home..."

Elizabeth's eyes lit up with sudden understanding. "Oh, is this about him submitting some artwork to the paper?"

Olivia's eyes widened, and she paused, then nodded. "...Yes. He's really good. Have you seen his drawings?"

"As a matter of fact, I have," Elizabeth said, trying not to shudder. The girls she had seen in his drawing were definitely her and Jessica. He'd captured their likenesses perfectly. It was kind of unnerving. She

Tobey's Story

wondered what the significance of the armor was, though. Some wisps of her earlier dream surfaced in her mind, and she tried not to blush. At least he hadn't drawn something like *that*...

* * *

Friday night finally arrived, but not without some difficulty. There was a project due in History, two tests, one in Chemistry and one in American Literature; and one quiz, in Spanish. Tobey turned in a project on the Burning Times—what he'd told Mr. Cato was actually partially true—and did his best on the tests. At least the Spanish quiz came naturally to him.

That evening, when Tobey had done all his homework and his chores, he lay in bed waiting until his mother was asleep so he could sneak up to the attic again. He flipped some pages in the book and consulted his notes on Latin pronunciation. It was near midnight when he was finally ready.

He sat on top of his father's trunk and opened the book, frowning as he looked once more at the diagram opposite the page with the Nyx woodcut. He'd thought the center symbol was the astrological symbol for Aries, but it wasn't.

It was something he'd never seen before, a rectangle divided in half vertically with an X through it, starting inside each corner:

Had he misread it the first time? He remembered the symbol being obscured by a stain, and now it was completely legible, no stain in sight.

His eyes travelled up and down the page, making sure that none of the other symbols were different than he remembered.

They weren't.

Well, it was now or never.

With shaking fingers, he drew the symbol in the center of the pentagram with the special chalk he'd found in his father's trunk. Then he stood up to survey his handiwork.

He found his left hand in the sleeve of his father's robe and, using the dagger, slashed across his right palm. He thought it would bleed more, but it made just a scratch. This was odd because he'd tested the sharpness of the blade the night before. It looked so easy in the movies... Wincing, he drew the dagger's blade across his palm once more, trying to deepen the scratch into a cut. Finally, he made a fist and managed to squeeze a drop of blood onto the center of the pentacle. His hand throbbed with pain.

His eyes widened as the symbols all around the outside of the pentacle began to glow purple. The center symbol glowed too, then seemed to sink into the floor and disappear, taking the tiny splash of blood with it.

Tobey drew back as purple smoke started billowing up through the floor, coming from the very center of the pentacle, where the rectangular symbol had been. He coughed and waved his hands in front of his face, trying to fan the smoke away so he could see. The smoke seemed to collapse in on itself, settling into the shadowy shape of a figure.

It was the silhouette of a woman, with glowing green eyes.

The female silhouette came into focus and then bloomed into full color, solidifying into an anthropomorphic being. It was a tall young woman with vibrant red hair, and a mysterious smile. She was wearing a long black dress and pointy-toed lace-up boots.

I did it! he thought. He'd summoned the demon! Only, it didn't *look* like a demon...

"Are you the Nyx?" he asked tentatively. *She's much too beautiful to be a demon,* he thought. Not only was she beautiful, but she looked *exactly* like the witch from his dreams.

Then he remembered that demons could take any form they pleased—the Nyx must've plucked the image of the glamorous witch out of his mind, taking that form to use against him. His heart started beating with a sickening thud. What exactly had he gotten himself into?

"Oh, dear," the demon said, her smile fading as she glanced at the pentacle marked on the floor around her. She looked at her own hands in confusion, then reached up to touch the sides of her head, as if feeling for something that was usually there, but was now absent. Then she looked him up and down. "This can't be good. And that accent is dreadful."

She didn't *sound* like a demon...

Tobey stared at her in bewilderment. "What do you mean? This is how I talk." Although he noticed that his jaw didn't ache like when he tried to talk to people at school.

"No, it isn't how you *taaalk*, Tobias, my darling," said the demon with a tinkling laugh.

Only his mother called him Tobias. He'd shortened it to Tobey once he'd started school, because the kids had made fun of him. *She knows my name,* he thought, getting chills up and down his arms. Then again, she was a demon. Demons were known to be very clever and devious. He'd have to tread carefully.

"Well, my mother was British, but living in Saccharin Valley all my life has given me an American accent," he told her.

Now it was *her* turn to stare at *him*. "'*Living in Saccharin Valley*'—?" she repeated incredulously. "Oh, Tobias, something is *very* wrong here."

The way she said his name made him tingle. He gazed at her reverently. "No, something is very right. Now that I've summoned you, you can help me get my revenge."

She paused to consider this, and her eyes gleamed. "Well, if it's a game, you know I'm always keen to play along. But why did it *have* to be Saccharin Valley? That's usually *my* schtick..."

"I don't know what you mean. Like I said, I've lived here all my life."

"But let me guess, you've always felt like an outcast?" the woman said, putting her hands on her hips. She had long nails, polished jet black.

"Yes, Mistress Nyx," he said. The demon seemed to know everything about him. It was exhilarating, and a little scary.

The woman winced a little. "Don't call me that," she snapped. "This is too weird."

"What can I call you, then?"

"Just call me Piper."

He shivered again. Piper was the name of the witch in his dream! Had he summoned her from the dream plane, or was this an evil demon in disguise as her? He didn't know.

The Nyx demon—*Piper*—glanced at the black candles he'd placed at each point of the pentacle. They were almost completely burned down. One flame started to sputter.

Tobey saw where she was looking and his eyes widened. How did the candles burn down so fast? The summoning magic must've used them up faster than normal.

"My time on this plane grows short," Piper said, in a booming voice that sounded more like what he imagined a demon would sound. "But I'm very *pleased* that you've summoned me." She looked at him for a long moment, a kind of sadness in her emerald eyes. In a more normal voice, she murmured, "We'll get you out of this, Tobias, don't worry."

Before he could ask what she'd meant by that, the candles all flickered out, and the demon disappeared into a plume of purple mist.

He sat back on the workbench, dazed. It had finally happened. He felt a delicious humming all throughout his body. He'd summoned a demon. If he'd done it once, he could do it again.

Of course, he'd have to keep cutting himself, he thought. He pulled the chain on one of the naked light bulbs hanging from the ceiling, and the light came on. He looked down at his right palm, which curiously did not hurt anymore, and gasped in surprise.

The slash wound had completely healed up. Now it was a faint pink line.

He picked up the crumbling old book, which was open to the demon-summoning spell, and looked at the

Tobey's Story

rendering of the demon again. She had slit-pupil eyes, sharp teeth, and ram horns curving around either side of her head.

He didn't mind that the demon had chosen to appear as the gorgeous dream witch, but he couldn't help but regret not being able to see her *true* form.

It was definitely a visage that could strike fear into his enemies.

He glanced at the pentacle, wondering if he should wipe it away. It was only drawn in chalk, after all. But then he looked at it and saw that it was already starting to fade. Maybe it was only good for one use. He'd have to draw it again for the next summoning.

His mother didn't come up into the attic very much—only to get the Christmas decorations once a year. Still, he felt relieved to be leaving no trace of his demon summoning.

He pulled off his father's robe and stuffed it back into the trunk, put the book in his backpack, turned out the attic light, and crept back downstairs.

Chapter 4

Galaxies away, in the Witch World, Piper awoke with a start, accidentally kicking one of the cats. "Sorry, Thora," she said to the gray cat, who glared at her, then started licking herself back in order.

"That was weird," Piper muttered. She'd been summoned as the Nyx demon—but showed up in human form. Or rather, witch form. But she'd been summoned from *Saccharin Valley*—by *Tobey*. Only he didn't look like his normal warlock self—he looked like a skinny, awkward high school student. He'd even had acne.

She glanced at his side of the bed. It was empty, and she could tell, using her Witch Sight, that he hadn't slept in it.

She got up to look in the bedroom down the hall. A witch's consort didn't *always* sleep in the same bed as his witch. Only on special occasions.

The bed was made, and there was no trace of his aura in the air. She frowned.

So Tobey really *was* in Saccharin Valley. Why? Saccharin Valley was *her* personal vendetta—

Jessica Wastefeld jumped out of bed. For once, she was happy to go to school, because the sooner school was over, the sooner she could get started on her weekend plans. She was *so* excited—

SACCHARIN VALLEY HIGH

"Hey!" Piper growled. "I'm trying to have a scene here!"

"You're not in this one," said the Omniscient Narrator.

"I am too," Piper said. "I was summoned."

"No, the *Nyx* was summoned," boomed the Narrator. "Besides, everyone knows that Jessica and Elizabeth are the main characters. So, where was I? AHEM!"

...Jessica took her dress out of the closet and hung it on the door. It was a kind of iridescent lavender color. It was beautiful, and she'd gotten it for a steal. It was as if the store appeared just for her...

"Rude," Piper grumbled from the Witch World. She magicked herself washed and dressed, and plodded into the workroom to do some divining. She needed more information if she was going to help Tobey...

"PAY ATTENTION TO ME!" Back in Saccharin Valley, Jessica yelled to the reader. "I'm very important to this story!"

"No, you're not," admonished the Narrator. "It says on the cover, *Tobey's Story*—"

"BUT WHAT DOES IT SAY BEFORE THAT?" Jessica yelled. "*SACCHARIN VALLEY HIGH*. Starring the Wastefeld twins—namely, ME!"

Elizabeth poked her head in the door of the bathroom they both shared. "What's all the yelling about?"

"I'm telling the narrator what's what," Jessica proclaimed.

"Jessica," Elizabeth chided, "You know this story is about someone else we go to school with. You don't have to throw a fit—we're still in the B-plot."

"B-plot, Schmee-plot," Jessica said dismissively. "We're supposed to be front and center. How about I show you my new dress? That's the important part of the story."

Elizabeth sighed and came into the room to look at the dress, dutifully agreeing that it was beautiful.

Tobey's Story

"Where did you get it?" she couldn't help but ask, even though she had to finish getting ready for school.

"A new store that I found downtown," Jessica said. "It's called Seraphina's."

"Hmm, I've never heard of that," Elizabeth said. "But 'Seraphina' means 'burning one' or 'fiery'..."

"I don't need a history lesson right now, Elizabeth," Jessica said scornfully. "I need the *bathroom!*" She pushed past her sister and took her place in the bathroom, slamming the door and locking it.

Elizabeth sighed as she realized she would have to go to school late, or on time, but without her face washed or her hair brushed.

That was Jessica for you.™

*   *   *

Saturday morning, Tom McLay, ace tennis player and Saccharin Valley's token gay, yanked open the door to The Book Cellar. He threw an old book on the counter. "It didn't work," he complained.

Mr. August, who had his back to him, slowly turned around. "What didn't work, my lad?" he asked pleasantly. "Nice to see you, by the way."

"The spell you gave me," Tom sulked. "I followed the book exactly. And then this guy transferred to my homeroom, and he was super cute, in a retro kind of way. But he wasn't... *like me,*" he finished in a low voice. He didn't think Saccharin Valley would let him say the word *gay* out loud.

"Oh? How could you tell?" Mr. August asked. ("Gaydar" was also not a word used in Saccharin Valley.)

"Every time I saw him, he was bent over a drawing of this girl. At first, I thought he was trying to throw people off, so no one would know he actually liked boys. So I talked to him, but he didn't seem interested at all." Tom scowled.

Mr. August had taken the book and was flipping pages. "When did you cast this spell?"

"About a week ago," Tom said. "Why?"

The shopkeeper found the page he was looking for and turned the book around so Tom could see. He tapped his finger on one line of small text. "Read this."

"For new beginnings, perform this ritual on the new moon," Tom read. He flushed. "Oh. I didn't see that part. It's my first foray into black magic, you know... I'm guessing the moon wasn't new a week ago?"

Mr. August shook his head. "Just past the third quarter, actually."

"So I could try again?" Tom asked hopefully. He looked at the calendar on the wall behind the counter and added excitedly, "The new moon is tonight!"

Mr. August looked worried. "I wouldn't recommend it. You've already upset the balance..."

"What balance?" Tom grumbled. "The one that prevents me from having a boyfriend in this podunk town?" He glanced around, wondering if he'd be struck by lightning for saying the word *boyfriend* so openly.

Then again, he was standing inside an occult bookstore, one that had popped up randomly for the sake of the plot, so it was probably OK.

"Wait at least another lunar cycle, to see if what you've previously set in motion resolves," Mr. August advised. "*Then* you can try again."

"Fine," Tom sighed. He took the book back from the store owner, and Mr. August handed him a Farmer's Almanac as well.

"Take this, and mind the moon before you enact any further spells," Mr. August said sternly.

"Yes, sir," Tom said. *I've waited this long, I suppose I can wait another 28 days.*

But once he got home, the man's dire words had faded from his mind. He lay on his bed, brooding. *I'd like at least to have a date for the dance,* he thought. *Even if we have to pretend to be just friends.*

He went into the bathroom to splash some water on his face, and when he looked in the mirror, he gasped. Someone else's face was superimposed over his own reflection—a good-looking boy with auburn hair and hazel eyes. The boy smiled at him.

Tobey's Story

I'm waiting for you, came a husky voice in his mind.

Tom got chills up and down his body. Was this his future boyfriend? He hadn't known he'd been gay long enough to glean if he had a type, but this boy seemed pretty cool. He could see muscular shoulders in the mirror, and wondered if the boy played tennis.

Tom started to say something to the boy in the mirror, but the glass fogged up, and when he wiped the fog away, all he could see was his own reflection.

He frowned at himself.

Pretty silly talking to a mirror anyway.

But then he went back into his bedroom, and saw that the book was open to the page with the spell he'd used the first time.

He felt a flutter in his stomach.

*   *   *

Tobey's mother was going on a business trip for the weekend. It had come up suddenly. At breakfast on Saturday, Mrs. North told him that her plane would leave shortly after lunch, and she had packed the night before. He was looking at the weather in the paper and realized the moon would still be mostly dark tonight.

Maybe he could summon the Nyx again.

"I know I can trust you not to have any rave-ups while I'm gone," she said with a smile.

"Of course," Tobey said.

"What are your plans, then? Any friends you can connect with?"

Tobey's blue eyes shone. "Yes, I did meet someone recently," he said evasively. *I summoned her through a pentagram in the attic.* "But on Sunday, I'll probably just stay home and study, do my chores, that sort of thing."

Mrs. North nodded. "I'll return on Monday evening," she said.

"Safe travels, then, Mother," he said, and gave her a kiss on the cheek.

As soon as she'd left for the Saccharin Valley airport, he grabbed his backpack and drove the Toyota downtown. He wanted to see Mr. August at The Book Cellar again.

There were no customers in the store, just like last time. Tobey briefly wondered if Mr. August *ever* had any customers... maybe they all came after the sun set.

"He returns," Mr. August said cheerfully. "What can I help you with?"

Tobey grinned. "I just wanted to thank you for the book. It worked."

Mr. August raised an eyebrow. "Oh? *What* worked, exactly?"

Tobey glanced around, even though he'd seen that they were the only people in the store. "I summoned a demon," he said in a low voice.

"Really?" Mr. August said offhandedly, turning away from Tobey to put something away in the locked glass case behind him.

Tobey had expected him to sound more impressed. After all, *magic was real*. Maybe the store proprietor knew this, but Tobey had just come upon this information.

Mr. August turned back around and looked at Tobey, his brow furrowed. "What did it look like?"

"She," Tobey corrected. "I mean, it *looked* like a woman. The woman I've been seeing in my dreams, actually."

"Demons often take the form of someone you know, to put you off your game," Mr. August said gravely.

"But I don't know Piper in real life," Tobey protested. "I've just been *dreaming* about her."

A look of concern came over Mr. August's eyes. "Then the demon plucked that image right out of your *head*," he told Tobey, his accent getting thicker. "You must be careful, not to let a demon into your mind..."

"Do you think I shouldn't try summoning her again?"

"*It*," Mr. August corrected. "Remember, this is an otherworldly being, not the woman of your dreams."

What if she's the demon *of my dreams?* Tobey thought. "Doesn't the fact that it's confined to the circle protect me from that kind of thing?" he asked.

Tobey's Story

"Usually," Mr. August told him. "Just don't ever give it permission to exit the circle, no matter what it tells you. Demons are cunning."

Tobey nodded, blowing out his breath. That seemed easy enough.

"You can summon it up to three times," Mr. August added.

"Thank you." He turned to leave, then stopped. "Oh, I almost forgot. The demon didn't stay very long. Almost immediately after I summoned it, the candles went out. How do I get her—*it*—to stay and help me?"

"Were the candles previously used?" Mr. August wanted to know.

"Yes," Tobey said. He didn't say by whom.

"It's better to use new candles," said Mr. August briskly. "And get taller ones, they burn slower."

Tobey nodded. "You've been a tremendous help to me."

The store proprietor smiled, showing one gold tooth in front. "Well, laddie, don't say I didn't warn you."

Tobey nodded and left.

As he came up the stairs, he noticed a home decor shop across the street.

He walked across the crosswalk—accidentally bumping into a girl on the way out, but not staying to chat—and went inside to buy five black taper candles. Actually, they were more of a stylish dark grey, but they were the darkest-colored candles in the store, so he hoped they would do. The store clerk, a cheerful woman in her 30s, looked suspicious, but rang him up without asking any questions.

He drove home, deep in thought.

* * *

"This is ridiculous," Jessica said. She had just gotten out of her car in the parking lot of Seraphina's. The store was still there, just as she'd thought. Looking down the street, she saw the same dry cleaner's and pet groomer's. What had Lila been talking about? There was no upscale boutique here.

She must've been on a different street, Jessica thought. Clearly, Lila was so used to being chauffeured everywhere that she didn't have the best sense of direction.

She'd wanted Lila to go with her, so she could prove her wrong, but Lila had declined, saying she had some sort of mysterious errand to run.

So Jessica had gone alone, if only to prove to herself that Seraphina's was real. The dress was still hanging in her closet, but it was *so* perfect, *so* magical, that she half expected to wake up and find that it had dissolved into mist, like a dream upon waking.

Jessica walked toward the store, but just then someone walking quickly in the other direction bumped against her shoulder.

"Watch where you're going!" she cried, rubbing her arm.

"S-sorry," the person mumbled. Jessica realized it was Tobey North, from school. He had an odd look on his face, and his stance was much more confident than usual.

In fact, he looked kind of... *handsome?*

"Oh, it's fine," she muttered, softening. How had she never noticed how beautifully blue his eyes were? And when had his acne cleared up? "Say, Tobey—"

"I've got to go." He spoke over her and was already walking away.

So rude, Jessica thought.

Then she put a hand to her face as she realized she'd almost *asked him to the dance.*

What was I thinking? she thought, watching the shy boy enter a home goods store across the street.

I must be losing my mind. The tiff between her and Lila was getting to her, she decided. She went up the walk to Seraphina's... but the store was closed.

On a Saturday? She peered through the glass of the door, but the store was dark, and she didn't see anybody inside.

Weird. She went back to her car. She had her dress for the dance, after all, and she would work on getting a date later. A week was plenty of time to snag someone awesome. Any day now, some gorgeous guy would fall out of the sky and be instantly smitten with her.

She was surprised it hadn't happened sooner, what with it being forty-some pages into the story...

Maybe I need to work on my tan. She pressed on the gas, deciding on the spur of the moment to go to the beach.

*   *   *

Lila pulled up to the upscale boutique. It was still here, and the space two stores down—where Jessica had said Seraphina's was—was still empty. But she wasn't interested in proving Jessica wrong anymore. She had an appointment with the owner, whose name was Maeve.

"Lila, good to see you, my dear," Maeve said. As soon as Lila was inside, she locked the door behind her. "Come in and have a cup of tea."

"Is he here?" Lila said expectantly.

"Patience," Maeve said with a throaty, cultivated chuckle. "Yes, he's on his way." She motioned for Lila to follow her behind the curtain and down a hall to a secret back room set up to look like an elegant parlor.

The boy she'd mentioned was eighteen years old, single, and gorgeous. He was her nephew, she'd said. He'd just graduated from Lovett Academy, and his parents were very rich.

Lila sat down to a formal tea service and chatted with the owner on tasteful subjects, like fine art, classic literature, and international cuisine.

When Rowan Berry finally arrived through the back entrance, he took Lila's breath away. He was tall and tanned, with chiseled features like a classical statue. He had long honey-blonde hair in a perfect blowout that made him look like Fabio, and large blue eyes similar to his aunt's.

"*Enchanté,*" he said, kissing her hand.

By the end of the afternoon, she had a date to the dance.

*   *   *

"Jessica!" Elizabeth scolded when her sister returned hours later. "Where have you been? You said you'd bring the car back in time for me to go to my study group. I had to get a ride with Todd."

Jessica took off her wide-brimmed hat and sunglasses. "Sorry," she said carelessly. "I lost track of time. Besides, who goes to a study group on *Saturday*?" She smiled, waved, and headed upstairs to her room.

Elizabeth sighed. She should've known Jessica would blow her off. Every time Jessica made a promise to her sister, Elizabeth held her to it, and then was surprised and angry when that promise was broken... but not for long, since they were twins and shared A Special Bond and whatever.

*   *   *

After dinner, when the dark moon was rising, Tobey went to the attic and drew the magic circle again, with the large pentagram inside that, the five symbols around the outside, and the rectangular symbol in the very center (double-checking to make sure it was the same as it was yesterday).

This time he poked the ring finger on his right hand with the point of the dagger, and let the blood drip onto the center of the pentagram.

The center symbol glowed and vanished, and he thought he saw the Aries symbol take its place—but then it too was gone.

What was that? he thought, feeling a flutter in his stomach. Had he done something incorrectly?

He kept going, reciting the incantation. Now that he'd done it once, he was feeling more confident in his chanting, and added extra oratory flair to the Latin words.

The shadow that rose from the center of the circle was taller this time. It had ram horns on each side of its head, with crimson curls tumbling over its shoulders.

Tobey's Story

Its eyes glowed yellow, not green. They were set in a nightmarish face with mottled green skin and demonic features.

His heart skipped a beat.

She was even more glorious than in the rendering. The sight of her took his breath away. He glanced at the taper candles, and they were still burning, with what looked like a long way to go.

As the demon came into focus, a grin spread on its face, full of pointed teeth. It was dressed in a long black gown with billowing sleeves, and spread its arms out, flexing claws.

The demon saw him, and a hissing noise escaped its lips as it looked him over.

This was definitely the Nyx. He dropped to his knees, bowing his head. He didn't know why; it just seemed like the thing to do.

The demon cupped his chin with a cold, clawed hand and tilted his face up to look at her.

"My l-lady," he stammered, gaping at her unnatural beauty. He wasn't sure how to address a demon.

"You may rise, Tobias, dear," rasped the Nyx. Her voice was much deeper than it had been the night before. He broke out in chills that were equal parts fear and pleasure.

He got to his feet.

"Why do you summon me, child?" the Nyx rasped. The sly smile on her demonic face made him think he had to be careful with his words, lest she twist them to use against him. He remembered what Mr. August had said. It was much easier to abide by the store proprietor's words when what he'd summoned looked like an actual demon.

"I seek p-power, O Great One," he said, hating the stammer in his voice. "I need your assistance in enacting revenge on my enemies."

"Enemies?" rumbled the demon. She waved a clawed hand, and a misty bubble appeared in the air at eye level. Inside the bubble, he could make out the forms of his bullies—Charlie Cashbox, Bruce Fatcat, and Kirk Danderson.

His eyes went wide. She'd plucked the images out of his mind again. *Careful,* he told himself.

"T-that's them," he said, stuttering again. Why was it so hard to speak all of a sudden? The American accent felt like a mouthful of rocks.

He thought about what she'd said the night before: *That accent is terrible.*

But it's not an accent. *It's how I talk.*

The bubble floating in the air vanished. The Nyx's eyes glowed brighter as she studied him. Perhaps she was reading his very thoughts.

"Speak, boy," she said, grinning. "Properly, this time."

Tobey felt a tingle in his throat, and he coughed to clear it. *Well, if she wants me to talk differently,* Tobey thought, *I shall.*

Somehow his thoughts sounded different in his head.

"Erm, sorry," he murmured. His ears perked up as he realized he didn't sound American anymore.

The rocks were gone from his mouth.

Also... his incisors felt a little sharper. "So, right then, I mean..." He cleared his throat, and began again. "Mistress Nyx, I summoned thee to smite my bullies," he said. "I'd be well-chuffed..." He couldn't help but laugh at the word choice from his new British accent. He wasn't sure he'd ever used the word *chuffed* before. Still, it felt right. Confidence swelled within him. "It would give me *great pleasure* if you were to enact my will...

"*Piper*," he finished, and the demon looked surprised, then pleased. "You told me to call you Piper, didn't you?" He marveled at the way the word "call" came out as "caul" and the *r* at the end of "Piper" had softened.

"So I did," Piper, the Nyx, replied. "I was trying to reach you in your dreams."

"That was you?" Tobey said incredulously. "I thought you were a witch..."

The Nyx nodded, not commenting on his last statement. *Maybe she wanted me to* think *she was a beautiful witch, so I'd summon her.*

Tobey's Story

But she's quite stunning as a demon... He supposed it didn't matter. Witch or demon, she was going to help him.

"Why do you need to get revenge on these mere mortals?" Piper the Nyx asked, her horned head cocked to one side. "You have tremendous power..."

"No, I bloody well don't," Tobey said, flushing with (British) anger. "I'm powerless. I'm a reject, a prat, and everybody at school is repelled by me. Unless, of course, they need to give someone a right pasting, then they all queue right up."

The Nyx gave him a once-over with her slit-pupil yellow eyes. "Yes, I see that," she drawled. "But I can take you away from here... away from infuriating Saccharin Valley, to a place where your rightful power will be restored."

Tobey licked his lips. "You mean... the Underworld?"

The demon laughed, and it gave him chills again. How he longed to laugh like that in the face of his bullies. But without the power the demon wielded, they'd just think he was nuts. *Especially if I start talking in this voice,* he thought. Charlie would definitely clobber him if he thought Tobey had a British accent all of a sudden.

But he could still talk like this to the Nyx. She understood him.

That'll be our secret, then, he thought.

"No, not quite the Underworld," the Nyx said. She looked like she was going to say more... but didn't.

Tobey clenched his fists. "Then, no, I'd rather stick around and put some *select* people in their places."

The Nyx smiled broadly, showing almost all of her jagged, yellow-white teeth. "Very well then," she said.

A feeling of great excitement bloomed in his stomach.

The demon held up one clawed hand, palm up, and a green flame appeared. It flickered, shrank, and burned down until it had gone out completely, leaving a small object in its place.

A black ring. "Wear this on your dominant hand," she instructed.

She handed it to him—her claws brushing against his hand made his insides melt—and he slipped it onto the middle finger of his left hand. It fit perfectly. "As long as you don't remove it, you will have power over your bullies."

"Thank you," he breathed.

"Don't thank me," she snarled. "You summoned me, I do your bidding."

"Right, well," he amended, in British. "Then... I license thee, Nyx, to depart?"

Even though he wasn't sure that phrase was correct, it seemed to do the trick. She nodded curtly and was enveloped in the tower of mist, vanishing back into the ether.

He looked at the candles. They were half burned down. How did that happen? He and the Nyx hadn't been talking long... but at least he'd gotten what he wanted.

He couldn't help thinking that he wanted to see her again.

But she's a demon, and I'm mortal...

Then he remembered that he could summon the Nyx one more time.

I will *see her again,* he told himself.

He was exhausted now, so he took off his father's robe, put it back in the trunk, and left the attic, shutting the door behind him.

As he collapsed into bed, imagining what tomorrow would be like, the ring felt warm.

Chapter 5

On that same night, Tom McLay was doing a spell of his own. But it wasn't for summoning a demon. He was attempting to summon a boyfriend, despite Mr. August's warnings about the "balance". It was the new moon, and he couldn't wait any longer.

His parents had gone out to eat, so he was home alone. He'd double-checked the spell to make sure he got everything right this time. There was no other fine print that he could see.

He went out to the patio. It was late, and the stars were out. He could see the moon too, shrouded in darkness. There was a slight breeze, and the temperature was balmy.

He lit the candle and spoke the words, just like he'd done the first time. Only this time he held the image of the cute boy he'd seen in the mirror in his mind.

When he finished the spell, the candle flame seemed to turn green, stretching toward the sky. Then there was a rumble of thunder in the distance, and a strong breeze blew the candle out.

That didn't happen the first time, he thought, shivering. It seemed colder all of a sudden, and dark clouds now covered the moon, obliterating it completely.

SACCHARIN VALLEY HIGH

He lit the candle again, so he could burn the piece of paper he'd written the spell on, tossing it in his father's grill so it could burn safely. Once it was reduced to ash, he took the candle and went up to his room.

Even though he wasn't sure the spell had worked this time, he could feel a little spark of excitement flare up in his stomach.

He fell into a deep sleep, and began to dream...

In his dream, there was a new student at Saccharin Valley High, but it was a girl. She was tall, with shoulder-length wavy red hair, green eyes, and full pouting lips. She was wearing the weirdest outfit he'd ever seen: a black dress, black-and-white striped stockings, and black Doc Martens. Her makeup was dark and creepy to match, and her jewelry was like a punk's: a spiker choker, a necklace of black beads with a black star charm, silver skull earrings, rings on all her fingers. Her nails were painted black, too.

She was the only person in homeroom when he entered. There was one light on in the classroom, and it shone directly on her like a spotlight. She looked confused, surveying her surroundings. Her brow furrowed when she saw him, as if trying to place him. Finally, her eyes lit up with recognition. "Tom? Tom McLay? Fancy meeting you here."

He blinked in confusion. "Do we know each other?"

"No... I guess we haven't met. Where's Tobey?" She had gotten up from the desk and walked over to the classroom's open doorway, peering out into the hall.

He followed her. There was no one in the hall. The school was empty, dark, and silent.

"Tobey North?" Tom McLay asked. "I don't know. We're not really friends..."

The girl turned to him, frowning. "Something's not right here."

"Hey, do you know...?" He was trying to ask about his boyfriend, but he couldn't think of his name. *I know his name, don't I? It starts with a P—*

"Do I know who?" The girl turned to look at him, frowning.

Tom sighed. "Never mind."

Tobey's Story

"I have to go," she said. "I have to find Tobey." She ran down the hall.

"Wait!" he called after her. Suddenly, it seemed very important to talk to her. He ran after her, but she disappeared at the end of the hall.

*   *   *

Tobey slept in on Sunday morning. He'd had blissful dreams all night—about the Nyx, and his newfound power. Of course, he hadn't tried it out yet. As he got dressed, he wondered what the best place would be to do that.

He could go get into a bar fight—but no one was at a bar on a Sunday morning. And he certainly wasn't going to seek out his bullies from school on a weekend.

It would have to wait until tonight, he decided.

In the meantime, there were plenty of chores and homework to do. He vacuumed his room, cleaned the bathrooms, and worked on a math assignment. It was menial work, but it went by fast because his mind was a million miles away.

Every time he walked by a mirror, he thought he saw a glimpse of glowing yellow eyes and a satisfied, sharp-toothed smile.

As the sun started to set, he put away his cleaning supplies and took a shower, then dressed in his most vintage-styled outfit, which was from the 20s, with a sweater vest and a newsboy cap. He didn't have to be ashamed of how he dressed anymore—no one would mess with him.

Or if they did, he'd be able to take care of it.

Pumped with excitement, Tobey drove to the seediest bar in Saccharin Valley, walked right inside, and ordered a beer, gazing steadily at the bartender. He could feel a prickling behind his eyes that seemed to indicate that the bartender wouldn't ask for ID—and he didn't, just filled a glass with what was on tap, looking slightly afraid.

SACCHARIN VALLEY HIGH

Rick Bendover, a sleazy dropout Jessica had one made the mistake of dating because she thought he'd seemed "dangerous," was at the end of the bar, nursing a drink he was also too young for, but only by a couple of years.

He sidled up to Rick and looked up at the old TV in the corner, which was playing a football game. "I say, barkeep, can we turn the telly to a *real* football game?" he said, making the British accent Piper had given him sound upper-class and silly.

The bartender grunted. "No, it stays."

"Pip, pip, then," Tobey said agreeably. "You American wankers *love* your game of pigskin."

Rick turned to him with a look of disgust on his handsome-yet-sketchy face. He looked Tobey up and down, taking in his retro outfit. "*What* did you say?"

"Oh, I meant no harm," Tobey said. "All in fun, there's a good chap."

Rick belched in his face.

Tobey exhaled, blinking, then pasted a smile on. "If you have something to say, my good fellow, perhaps we can take it outside?"

Rick didn't need to be asked twice.

The fight was exhilarating. Tobey let Rick punch him once, and felt no pain. His split lip healed up immediately, and Rick paused, confused.

"What the hell..." he began.

Then Tobey's eyes began to glow.

"Go on, give it another go," he said encouragingly. He could hear a dangerous undertone to his voice that thrilled him.

"You got it," smirked Rick, having recovered from seeing his victim's wound heal up in real time. He swung again, but this time Tobey deflected Rick's arm by pushing up his own, then caught Rick's fist and twisted it behind his back.

"Let me go, you Limey freak," Rick growled.

"If you say so," Tobey said pleasantly. He did so, and Rick glared at him for a moment, looking like he

Tobey's Story

wanted to land another blow, then merely spat on the ground and stalked back inside the bar.

Tobey giggled delightedly. He couldn't wait to tell the Nyx—*Piper*—how his little outing had gone.

He turned to leave, but the bartender, who was standing in the doorway, whistled sharply. "Hey, fancy-pants, come in and pay your tab, and then I'm kicking you out," he said. "I'm not having any out-of-town punks starting fights in my bar."

Tobey's eyes glowed blue again. "Technically, we were outside... and *Rick* started it."

As if hypnotized, the bartender made an about face, disappeared inside, and then reappeared dragging Rick by the collar. "Beat it," he growled.

"All right, all right, no need to get your panties in a twist," Rick muttered. The door slammed behind him, and he looked at Tobey. "This isn't over, Limey."

"Oh, will there be more?" Tobey asked excitedly. "Looking forward to it." He sauntered over to his car and drove away, pushing up a cloud of dust that blew up in Rick's face.

*   *   *

Jessica was having a very strange dream on Sunday night. She was in her nightgown, sitting on a cold stone floor. Sitting up, she realized she was inside of a huge pentacle marked on the floor in what looked like dried blood. She froze, her heart thumping in her chest.

"You're awake," came a deep, velvet voice.

"Who's there?" Jessica said. The light was dim, and there were torches set high in the wall, casting ever-changing shadows about the room, which had no windows.

One of the shadows was the shape of a person, wearing a dark blue robe with the hood pulled over his or her head.

"So nice to see you, Jessica, dear," said the voice. It was male and had a British accent. "I was just sacrificing—*talking to*—your sister the other night."

"Who are you?" Jessica cried, stumbling to her feet, wincing as the cold bit into the skin of her bare feet. "Show yourself!"

"As you wish," the figure said, pulling the hood down. The face underneath was a handsome sorcerer with cold blue eyes and a goatee.

He looked like Tobey North, but older, and strangely attractive.

"Stay away from me!" Jessica yelled.

Lighting bolts came streaking in from both sides of her, hitting her wrists. She winced and cried out—and when she looked down, she saw that she was now chained to the wall.

A second figure emerged from behind the first. "I'll take care of her, darling," purred a familiar female voice.

Piper, Jessica thought. Then she frowned, wondering who the hell *Piper* was.

The new figure also pulled down its hood—but instead of a redheaded witch, it was the most handsome boy she'd ever seen. A smile spread across his rugged face, and his hazel eyes glinted.

"Who *are* you?" Jessica asked, her eyes wide.

*   *   *

Monday morning, Tobey awoke five minutes before his alarm went off. He got up and examined himself in the mirror. No cuts, no bruises—he was fresh as a daisy. He'd even grown a little stubble on his upper lip.

"Many thanks, Piper," he said to the mirror in the same British accent as last night.

The eyes of his reflection glowed green for a moment.

There was traffic on the way to school, and he ended up missing homeroom. But that was fine with him, as he wouldn't have to deal with Jessica Wastefeld's disgust, or Elizabeth Wastefeld's pity.

He *had* hoped to run afoul of Charlie Cashbox's bullying, but then, he had the whole school day ahead of

Tobey's Story

him. It would be *very* interesting to see what would happen.

*   *   *

In homeroom, Jessica and Lila were informed that there was a new student—a broad-shouldered, ginger-haired boy named Quentin Pepper. Jessica thought that name was ridiculous, so she didn't look up when the teacher announced that he would be attending Saccharin Valley High.

But then Lila whispered, "Wow." Jessica followed her friend's gaze to the front of the room, where the boy was standing, shuffling his feet a little and looking at the back wall, as if he didn't want to meet any of his new classmates' eyes.

Quentin Pepper was gorgeous. He had hazel eyes, short, wavy reddish-brown hair, and a dimple in his chin. His jawline was strong, and his cheekbones to die for. He was wearing a dark green Henley shirt and khakis.

He looked a little out of place. Jessica began to pay attention to what the teacher was saying.

"Quentin just moved here from Santa Rosa," she said brightly. "But he was born and raised in Kilmarnock, Scotland. Isn't that interesting?"

The students mumbled with little enthusiasm.

Only Jessica said in a clear, audible voice, "Oh, yes!"

Everyone in the class turned and looked at her. Lila snickered.

She blushed.

"Quentin, could you teach us any words or phrases in a *Scottish burr*?" the teacher went on, attempting a Scots accent, which fell a little flat.

A look of disgust briefly crossed Quentin's face. He glanced at the window in the classroom. "Well, the weather's a wee bit *dreich* for Southern California," he said finally. "That means *dreary*," he added, realizing he'd need to explain a bit more based on the class's blank looks.

Jessica noticed his voice was just low enough to be sexy—not like those geeks who hadn't gone through puberty yet—without sounding unintelligible or like a dumb jock. (Although she did go for a dumb jock on occasion. Since they were so dumb, they were easier to bend to her will.)

"*Aye*, it is," the teacher said enthusiastically, making the new boy wince. "But don't worry, it'll be back to sunny and perfect in no time."

Quentin nodded listlessly and took a seat at an empty desk near the window in the third row. Jessica could see him looking furtively at all the other students—it almost looked like he was trying to locate someone specific.

She noticed that Tobey North was absent, but she wasn't concerned. *Elizabeth* would have been concerned, had she been there, but she was in the *Oracle* office.

Seeing him look around, she thought, *He must be looking for the gorgeous blonde in the back.* She wanted to wave at him and say, "Over here!"

But Jessica wasn't the type of girl to throw herself at a guy (or so she thought, despite much evidence to the contrary). She'd play it cool, and he'd be eating out of her hand by lunchtime.

"Yum," Jessica whispered to Lila. "I call dibs."

"You can have him," Lila said. "With a wardrobe like that, I'm not interested. Besides, he probably eats haggis."

"He was only *born* in Scotland," Jessica argued. "He probably doesn't remember any of it. At least he doesn't wear a kilt!" She giggled.

When the bell rang, she shot up from her seat, trying to catch up with him, but he had exited the classroom swiftly. She paused just outside the door, scanning the halls for a ginger head—but she couldn't find him.

Drat, she thought. *Why are you playing hard-to-get, Quentin Pepper?*

Every class Jessica had up until lunch was utterly boring and depressing—mostly because Quentin wasn't in any of them. Jessica was about to fall asleep in her math class when Cara poked her.

When it was finally time for lunch, she joined her friends, Lila, Cara, and the other cheerleaders. They were all telling each other excitedly about dresses they'd found for the dance, and the dates they'd gotten.

"What about you, Jess?" Cara said, slurping her diet soda.

Jessica realized to her dismay that she was the only one at the table who didn't have a date. It was practically unheard of for her. She was co-captain of the cheerleading squad, a member of the exclusive sorority Pi Beta Alpha, and, according to her, *the* best-dressed girl in school. If word got out that she didn't have a date, all the school's unwashed miscreants and losers would flock to her, clamoring for a date. *At least I already rejected Tobey North,* she thought. She wouldn't have to deal with him.

She hadn't admitted it to her sister, but he'd seemed weirdly familiar to her. Especially when he'd bumped into her downtown. (She'd decided she'd been seeing things when she'd thought he'd suddenly turned handsome. When glimpsing him in the hall today, he'd gone back to normal: sullen, greasy-faced, and awkward.)

"Well," Jessica said, trying to sound chipper, "I found the most *gorgeous* dress at this new store downtown. You should see it. It's fabulous, and I got it for a steal."

"And I got *my* dress at the upscale boutique that Jessica insists doesn't exist," Lila interrupted.

Jessica looked annoyed. "I told you, you must've gotten your streets mixed up. *My* store was called Seraphina's."

"And mine was called Rowan. This very chic, elegant woman helped me find the perfect dress," Lila said. "She knows the designer Pierre Delacroix *personally*... Wait'll you see it. It's emerald green, and to die for."

"I can just imagine," said Sandra Back-Bacon. "And who's the lucky guy, Jessica? You didn't mention him."

Jessica blushed slightly. "I haven't decided yet. I want to be very careful in my selection."

"You don't have a date?" Lila said. "That's terrible." Her voice was sympathetic, but her brown eyes were gleaming, as if Jessica's lack of date was the best news she'd heard all day. Lila and Jessica were extremely competitive. It was a wonder they'd been friends as long as they had.

"But I have several very good choices, as far as I'm concerned," Jessica went on casually. "Top of my list is the new boy."

"Tobey North?" Jean Chest said with a frown.

Jessica shot her friend an annoyed look. "What? No. I wouldn't date that creep if he was the last guy on Earth. I meant Quentin... Quentin Pepper." Saying his name aloud, it still sounded absurd... but then she remembered his broad shoulders and handsome features.

"Oh, he's *very* cute," Cara said. "But he's also very mysterious. Usually, Caroline has all the latest, but even *she* didn't know anything more about him than what the teacher said."

"Well, I bet you by the end of the day, I'll know everything there is to know about him," Jessica said, smiling confidently at Lila.

Lila just rolled her eyes. "My date for the dance doesn't go here—he's the wealthy nephew of the store clerk at Rowan. The store's actually named after him. *Rowan*—such a classy name." She sighed dreamily.

Jessica narrowed her eyes. Lila hadn't mentioned a date until just now. "I'll believe it when I see it."

The other girls kept on chattering and eating, and Jessica picked at her salad, watching everyone who came through the cafeteria doors. She saw her sister enter with Enid and join the lunch line.

Todd, Winston Eggbret, and Ken Cashews had already gotten their food and were sitting at a table near the door.

Finally, Quentin Pepper sauntered in. He took Jessica's breath away. Despite the boring, conservative way he dressed, there was an air about him that was mysterious and alluring. It seemed like everyone was looking at him when he appeared.

"Yo, Quentin!" Winston called. "Come sit with us."

But Quentin walked right by them.

Jessica's heart skipped a beat as he approached her table. She sat up straight and shot him a dazzling smile.

But he didn't meet her gaze and walked right past her—toward a table at the back, where Tobey North was sitting alone. Tom McLay had just gotten up from the seat across Tobey, a frown on his face, and he was hurrying away.

Jessica watched in dismay as Quentin took the seat Tom had just vacated, as if he and Tobey were already acquainted. They must've met in one of their morning classes because Tobey had been absent from homeroom.

What could they possibly have in common? She fumed. She decided to go through the dessert line, which conveniently came out near the table Tobey was sitting at. With any luck, when she came out, Tobey would be gone and she'd have Quentin all to herself.

* * *

Tobey looked up in surprise as a new boy he didn't recognize joined him at his loner table, acting as if they were already friends.

"How's it going, Tobias?" the boy asked in a friendly tone. His eyes were hazel, but the shape of them seemed oddly familiar to Tobey. The rest of him was *very* good-looking, but since Tobey tended to not get along with the super-handsome crowd, it was doubtful that they knew each other.

"It's Tobey," Tobey muttered.

The boy held out a hand to shake. "Tobey, right. I'm new here. My name is Quentin."

Tobey shook his hand unenthusiastically. "How did you know my name?" he asked, taking care to speak in an American accent, as he'd been doing all morning in his classes. It didn't feel like rocks in his mouth anymore—it felt like a delicious secret between him and the Nyx.

"I asked Jessica Wastefeld," Quentin said with a gleam in his eyes. He set a brown paper bag lunch on the table.

"No doubt she told you I'm a hideous freak," Tobey replied shortly. "So I can't help but wonder what you're doing here."

Quentin's smile faded. He seemed to be thinking very hard about what he wanted to say next. "Well... I could tell right away, Jessica is a superficial twat."

Tobey let out a squawk of laughter at the British insult. No one ever said that word around here. He half expected a teacher to come up and reprimand Quentin... or maybe a gym coach, with a whistle. *Fifteen laps for using that word!* "You've got that right," he muttered. "And her sister—"

"*So* sanctimonious," Quentin interjected.

Tobey stared at him. "Yes. How do you know so much, if you just got here?"

"I have a sort of sixth sense," Quentin said evenly, watching Tobey's reaction.

Tobey didn't say anything, just looked at him dubiously.

"It was something I was born with, although I honed this skill with a book from The Book Cellar," Quentin went on. "Do you know it?"

Tobey's eyes widened in surprise, then narrowed in suspicion. It was an odd coincidence that the new boy had recently found the bookstore that Tobey had just happened upon himself. He wasn't sure he could trust Quentin... but one look in his eyes told him that it was OK. Quentin seemed friendly, and Tobey hadn't had a real friend since grade school.

"I've been there," Tobey said. "Mr. August sold me a book about—"

Before he could go on, Bruce Fatcat sauntered up. "Quentin Pepper," he said. "You're a hard man to track down. What are you doing with this loser? Why don't you join me at *my* table?"

"Bruce Fatcat," Quentin responded. Tobey watched the exchange tersely. Would his new friend abandon him, or stick up for him? Not that he needed anyone to stick up for him anymore, since he was wearing the ring the Nyx had given him. His middle finger tingled at this thought. Maybe—

"I've heard a lot about you," Quentin was saying to Bruce. "Yes, it seems like I *am* a little mixed up on my first day at school here..." He laughed good-naturedly.

"You got that right," Bruce snickered. "Come on, I brought a meal prepared by my personal chef—this cafeteria food isn't even good enough for pig slop."

Quentin got up, and Tobey felt utterly rejected.

But as the new boy left, he dropped a crumpled piece of paper on the table, surreptitiously behind his back.

Tobey waited until they'd gone, then snatched up the paper.

Fatcat is a sodding git, it read. (Another British insult, Tobey noted.) *There are spies everywhere. Meet me after school under the big oak if you want to talk about the Occult.*

When had Quentin had time to write this? Did his 'sixth sense' inform him that he'd be poached from Tobey's table by Bruce? Tobey was mystified.

He glanced around to make sure no one had seen him, then he thrust the note into his pocket.

*   *   *

"This food is fantastic," Quentin said, taking a bite of pan-fried sole with lemon and capers. They were sitting at a table in the far corner of the cafeteria, which was partially hidden from view by a large potted plant.

"I know," Bruce bragged. "I have it imported special every day, just for me... and select other people of my choosing."

"It was so nice of you to invite me to your *exclusive* table," Quentin went on.

"Well, I could tell when I met you, you travel in the same circles as I do," Bruce said.

Quentin leaned in close. "Maybe you'd like to go somewhere private and discuss this further," he said in a low voice. He reached across the table and delicately wiped the corner of Bruce's mouth with his own napkin, his eyes gleaming like topaz.

Bruce jerked away. "*What are you doing?*" he hissed, shoving Quentin back into his seat. He straightened his collar nervously. Quentin could see him turning red, and then taking a deep breath to compose himself, glancing around to make sure no one had seen.

"My apologies," Quentin said in a husky voice. His eyes were half-lidded, like a satisfied cat's. "I thought you were gay, because, you know... you're so *pretty* and well-groomed."

Bruce huffed to himself. Sure, he was pretty, he knew that, but having another student—a *male* student—tell him that made his stomach churn.

Then he noticed the stud in the other boy's ear. He stood up quickly, stunned, then angry, and grabbed the other boy by the collar.

"I'm *rich*," he said through gritted teeth. "Not a *homo*."

"Of course," Quentin said, giving Bruce an ingratiating smile. Bruce let go, and stared at Quentin with his lip curled, as if he was utterly repulsed by the sight of him.

Quentin brushed some crumbs off his pant legs. Bruce saw that his nails were a little long and... polished?

"Look, this stays between us, OK?" Bruce told him menacingly. "I have a reputation to maintain..." He reached for his wallet and pulled out a few twenties, sliding them over to Quentin. Money was always helpful in smoothing things over, he knew.

Quentin's lips stretched in a broad smile. "As you wish." He gathered up the cash, slid it into his back pocket, and sauntered out of the cafeteria.

Bruce shut his eyes so he wouldn't be looking at the other boy's butt as he left.

Chapter 6

Tom McLay didn't see the new boy until after lunch. He'd left the cafeteria after trying to talk to Tobey one more time—he wanted to be absolutely certain Tobey wasn't the one. Today Tobey had seemed more confident, almost arrogant. His voice sounded a little different, and he kept fiddling with a ring on his left middle finger.

Tobey clearly wasn't the boy Tom had summoned. Or if he was, he wasn't the sort of boy Tom would like to date. Maybe because Tom had performed the ritual under the wrong moon phase, his dream boyfriend had come out... straight.

But since he'd done the spell again under the new moon, something *had* to happen. All morning he'd been on the lookout for any new faces.

As the students filed into Mr. Russo's chemistry class, a broad-shouldered boy with hazel eyes and reddish-brown hair sauntered in. He was looking around the classroom, and their eyes met briefly.

Tom sat up very straight, his heart thumping in his chest.

It almost looked like the boy's eyes were glowing.

"We have a new student joining us today, so let's all make him feel welcome," Mr. Russo said. "Quentin Pepper, did you enjoy our lovely cafeteria?"

SACCHARIN VALLEY HIGH

"Um, sure," Quentin said. He was still looking at Tom, who noticed that there was a small earring in the boy's right ear. His heart fluttered in his chest.

"Since Mr. McLay's usual lab partner is absent, why don't you pair up with him?" Mr. Russo suggested, gesturing at the empty stool next to Tom. Up close, the new boy looked *exactly* like the reflection he'd seen in his mirror the night before last.

Quentin took his seat. "Thanks for putting up with me," he said with a shy smile. "I'm not well-versed in chemistry... I'm more into sports than science."

"No worries, man," Tom said, his eyes lighting up. "Do you play tennis?"

*   *   *

Piper Quintin almost went into the girls' bathroom after class, before remembering that she was a dude. How had her travel spell to Saccharin Valley gone so wrong? Not that she didn't enjoy making Jessica lust after her, and throwing Bruce off his game. But she'd expected this trip to be a simple retrieval operation. She wasn't sure how Tobey had ended up here, or why he looked like a pubescent American loser. Not just any American loser—he seemed to think that he was a Southern Californian high school student, which was very incorrect.

But at least he'd found the occult bookstore, and been given the book that could summon her... in *demon* form. Now that her corporeal form was in Saccharin Valley, he would no longer be able to summon her, either as a witch or as a demon.

Piper washed her manly hands in the sink, noting that several boys simply urinated and left. Gross. She had to focus on the task at hand. Namely, getting Tobey to trust Quentin so she could make him remember who he was.

She remembered the last time a stint in Saccharin Valley had involved amnesia—it was Aetemus who'd banished her to Saccharin Valley without her memory or her witch powers. Tobey had dutifully dove in after her, and they'd gotten it sorted out... eventually.

Tobey's Story

But this scenario didn't *feel* like Aetemus's doing. There was something else going on. So she'd played along when Tom McLay started hitting on Quentin. Maybe he had something to do with it—

"REMEMBER ME?" Jessica shrieked, interrupting yet again to hijack the narrative. "I'm your friendly neighborhood main character—drop-dead gorgeous to boot—and I'm taking control of this C-plot!"

Jessica had gone over to Bruce Fatcat's table to insinuate herself to Quentin at lunch, but he'd shooed her away. She and Bruce had had a fling once upon a time, but she'd lost her entire identity trying to be someone Bruce would like, and it had gotten exhausting after a while. Bruce was so full of himself.

She thought she'd catch Quentin after lunch, but by the time she was done eating, he'd already left to go to his next class.

Luckily, Jessica found another opportunity in her very last class of the day—French, with Ms. Dalton. Elizabeth wasn't in this class, and neither was Lila, so Jessica would have no distractions from going after what she wanted.

She waited until Ms. Dalton told the class to select partners to go over vocabulary words, and shot out of her seat to take the empty desk next to Quentin.

"*Bon après-midi,*" Jessica said breezily. "*Je m'appelle* Jessica Wastefeld. You're in my homeroom class, aren't you?"

"*Tu me fais shier,*" Quentin muttered.

Jessica's smile faltered. "*Pardon,* I didn't catch that," she said.

"Yes, Jessica. I remember. You have a twin sister named Elizabeth, right?" Quentin went on smoothly.

"Yeah, but she's not like me at all," Jessica said. "She likes to stay home and read, but *I* like to party..."

"*En français!*" Ms. Dalton ordered, walking by their desks.

Jessica giggled. She scrambled for her textbook. "*Le cahier*, notebook," she said dutifully to her partner.

"*Le livre,* book," he responded. "*Le pupitre,* desk."

Once Ms. Dalton had moved on, she scribbled a note to him with *le stylo*.
We're having a dance this Friday. Do you have a date?
Quentin's hazel eyes sparkled.

*   *   *

Gym class was vastly different for Tobey now that he had the ring. Suddenly he was very athletic. During warm-up exercises, he did the most pull-ups he'd ever been able to do, and he ran laps in record time.

Several boys seemed surprised, and Coach Schultz was impressed. "Looks like you've been working on your upper body strength," he commended.

Tobey kept the ring on while he showered. He didn't want to lose track of it.

When he'd gotten dressed again, Charlie Cashbox was waiting for him, with his arms crossed and a menacing scowl on his face.

Tobey broke into a grin. *Bring it on,* he thought.

He left for his next class without a scratch on him, but Charlie, on the other hand...

Once the bell rang at the end of the day, all the high-school kids streamed out of the school's front doors and down the steps. Tobey pushed past several people moving too slowly for his taste and hurried around the side to the oak tree to meet Quentin. He could see the broad-shouldered boy in silhouette standing behind the tree, facing away from him.

He turned around when he heard Tobey coming. "You made it," he said, with a smile.

Tobey had thought Quentin's eyes were hazel, but in the sunlight, they looked bright green, like newly mown grass.

"How did lunch with *Bruce* go?" Tobey wanted to know.

"Terrible," Quentin said cheerfully. "Somehow, he was under the impression that *I* was rich too... I don't

Tobey's Story

know *what* gave him that idea... When he found out I wasn't, he lost interest."

Tobey's eyes sparkled. He marveled at the way Quentin could take control of a situation. He wondered what kind of book Quentin had found at Mr. August's store.

"So, uh—" here Tobey darted looks to his left and right to make sure no one was around—"you went to that occult bookstore?"

Quentin nodded. He rummaged through his black backpack, which he'd set on the grass under the tree. "That's where I got this."

Tobey's eyes widened as he looked at the cover. It was the same *Witchcraft* book that Mr. August had given him! Did that mean Quentin's "sixth sense" was a wish granted to him by a demon he'd summoned?

"I know this book," Tobey said excitedly. "I have a copy just like it." He took the book and flipped through it—then frowned. The table of contents in Quentin's book was different than his. The chapter headings were stuff like "The Third Eye," "Divination," and "Communicating with Animals,"... there was no section on summoning demons that he could see. "Huh," he said. "Mine doesn't look like this inside..."

"Really? That's weird. Do you want to come over to my house and compare notes?"

Tobey started to say yes, but then remembered his mom was coming home this afternoon and he'd shirked some of his chores when he'd tried the ring out the day before. "I can't, I'm sorry," Tobey said, picking up his own backpack. "Maybe tomorrow? I have stuff I have to do at home..."

"Tomorrow, then," Quentin said, with an easygoing smile that didn't match the concerned look in his eyes. "Here's my number in case you want to call me." He handed Tobey a slip of paper.

Tobey put the paper in his pocket. "See you," he said, and walked off.

Charlie seethed as he watched Tobey leave the school grounds after talking to the new boy—they seemed to be comparing notes for homework or something. He wanted to march over and dump the book out of that smug boy's hands, but he'd bide his time. In gym class, Tobey had been decidedly strong and athletic all of a sudden. He'd given Charlie a black eye.

Charlie briefly wondered if he'd been hustled. How else could you explain Tobey's sudden change in agility?

This isn't over, Freak, he thought. He wasn't going to let Tobey get away with what he'd just done.

But he might need some help in putting Tobey in his place.

He spotted Aaron Dulles, a soccer player with an anger problem. "Hey, Dulles," he called.

*   *   *

When Tobey got home, he dropped his backpack at the foot of his bed and dug into his jeans pocket for Quentin's number—but it wasn't there. He checked all his other pockets, but only came up with lint.

I must've lost it on the way home, he thought. His chest tightened, and then he realized he would still see Quentin at school.

He checked his middle finger to make sure he still had the ring. He was still wearing it, but decided to remove it for cooking dinner.

He placed the ring in a carved wooden box on his dresser. He'd had the box since he was little—his dad had given it to him before he left.

Then he slipped his copy of *Witchcraft* into his backpack and went downstairs to the kitchen.

*   *   *

Quentin found the car he assumed was his (it was the only Jaguar in the parking lot), and drove to a house that seemed like it was the right one. To his surprise, it was a charming three-story Victorian, just like back home.

Tobey's Story

He pulled up the drive, which went around the back of the house, and opened the door he found there. Yes, this kitchen seemed familiar. There was food in the fridge, and he started to make himself a snack. But then he decided to see if anyone else was home.

He looked in all the rooms, but there were no parents or siblings anywhere. *Fine with me,* he thought. (Based on his previous experience, Saccharin Valley versions of his family would be creepy.) The bedroom that seemed to be his was on the third floor, in the tower room, at the top of a narrow set of stairs.

There was a fantastic view up here—he could see the rest of the neighborhood nestled in the valley, and the mountains in the distance.

He did notice it was very much a boy's room. There was a plain double bed with a wooden headboard and hunter-green comforter, an old chair with a plaid throw blanket over it (it was the MacLeod tartan, he noticed), and a dark wood desk. All masculine except for one thing: in the corner was a vanity table with a lighted mirror.

He switched on the lights for the vanity. When he looked in the mirror, he saw a 17-year-old witch with shoulder-length wavy red hair and emerald eyes, wearing a black dress. He grinned at his reflection.

Maybe he could be himself here. If not bodily, then in spirit.

After inspecting the tiny attached bathroom and the closet (which was filled with snazzy yet decidedly male clothing), he went down to the parlor with the *Witchcraft* book.

He'd lied when he told Tobey it was from The Book Cellar. In fact, it had just appeared in his backpack. The name of the store was stamped inside the front cover. And inside of the back cover, someone had stuffed some extra pages torn out of a similar book.

The pages were instructions on how to summon a specific demon—the Hellcniht.

There was a rendering on one of the pages. The "Hellcniht" looked very familiar, he realized.

Here goes nothing.

SACCHARIN VALLEY HIGH

*   *   *

That night, Tobey had a completely different dream than usual. It wasn't just the lack of the red-headed witch—the whole feel of the dream was odd. It was almost as if he were eavesdropping on someone else's dream.

He was not in the dream himself, or at least, he didn't seem to have a body. But he did have a consciousness and eyes with which he watched the dream, as if it were a movie on a screen.

Quentin Pepper was drawing a pentacle on a wooden floor in an old house. It was very similar to the one Tobey had used for the Nyx.

However, the symbols around the outside of the pentagram were different. The words were still in Latin, but they were not the exact same words he had used.

Smoke poured out of the center of the pentacle, but it was blue this time. The smoke enveloped Tobey's incorporeal form, and he lost consciousness.

When he came to, he was standing in the center of the pentacle. *Wait, this can't be right,* he thought. He looked down and saw that he was wearing a charcoal suit with a sapphire-blue shirt.

At the end of his shirt sleeves were two peculiar-looking hands—they were red-skinned with long knobby fingers and black claws. He gasped and glanced over at a mirror on the parlor wall.

His face wasn't his—it was the face of a demon, with leathery red skin, wicked features, yellow slit-pupil eyes, and bullish black horns.

He gaped at his visage. It was horrifying... yet familiar.

He turned to his summoner. Quentin Pepper had gone all misty around the edges and was transforming into someone else—Piper, the red-headed witch.

"Who *are* you?" he cried. His voice came out deep and silky like a very *refined*, British-accented demon.

"Sorry," the witch said. "I wasn't sure if this would work."

Tobey's Story

Tobey found himself growling at her. Instead of being scared, she looked thrilled.

"Oh, maybe I can do something with this," she murmured.

Blue smoke towered up from the center of the pentacle. A misty shape of a figure, tall and lean with bull horns, started to appear.

Quentin could make out two yellow eyes, and then the candles sputtered and went out.

The figure vanished.

"Dammit, Tobey," Quentin muttered. He'd figured out that if he didn't think of himself as Piper, he could fool the narrator into thinking he was an important part of the plot. After all, Jessica Wastefeld had found Quentin to be super dreamy, and she was one of the two main characters.

Therefore, Quentin was a main character by association.

But summoning Tobey as a demon hadn't worked. He'd have to try talking to the mortal, high-school student iteration of Tobey again tomorrow.

He went downstairs to make himself dinner. It was awfully lonely in this house with no parents. There weren't even any pets.

While he was eating, he pored over the book, hoping it could give him some clue. After reading the chapter on "The Third Eye," he found that he could spy on Tobey by grounding and centering himself, and closing his two eyes... while opening the third, the invisible one in the center of his forehead, that aligned with the pineal gland inside his brain.

Tobey was cooking dinner, so that wasn't very interesting. Quentin read on. The chapter on "Communicating With Animals" was good, except that he realized why he didn't have any pets. A quick peek out the back door confirmed there weren't any birds or squirrels in the yard, either. It was empty and silent. The sun was setting, and the final day of the waning moon was rising.

SACCHARIN VALLEY HIGH

In Saccharin Valley, the moon, his old friend, looked wrong.

When it was time for bed, he trudged back up to the tower room, wishing he had a cat or a witch's consort to cuddle up with.

He slept without dreams.

Chapter 7

The next morning Tobey was late for homeroom *again*—he wasn't sure how this kept happening—and since he didn't have any classes with Quentin, he decided to meet him at lunch at the same table from the day before. Quentin looked relieved to see him.

"Did you bring your copy of the book?" he asked in a low voice. Mercifully, their table was in a far corner of the cafeteria, and everyone else was focused on their own lunch, so they had some privacy. Tobey did notice that Quentin kept glancing over his shoulder, in the direction of where Jessica was sitting... and then over his other shoulder, at Tom McLay, who was sitting with some of his tennis mates.

"Yes," Tobey said, sliding it out of his backpack and placing it on the table. "Sorry I missed you in homeroom. There was traffic, again."

"It's OK," Quentin said with an affable smile. "But why didn't you call?"

"Oh... I lost your number," Tobey said, embarrassed.

Quentin gave a little laugh and scribbled his number on another scrap of paper. He handed it to Tobey, then went on, "I had to fend off some advances from Jessica. She's got her sights set on me, for some reason."

"She's always on the prowl," Tobey replied, his eyes gleaming as he tucked the scrap of paper in his jacket pocket. "For boys she deems *cute*, at least." Tobey wished he could've been there to see Quentin turn Jessica down.

Quentin had taken Tobey's copy of the book and placed it next to his, with both of them open to the Table of Contents. He skimmed both books' content pages, looking back and forth between them. "Wow," he said. "Your book *is* different than mine. Have you actually tried any of this stuff?"

Tobey swallowed nervously. He still wasn't sure he could trust Quentin... but they both had a book from The Book Cellar about witchcraft, and that couldn't be just a coincidence.

"I did," he said at last, in a hushed tone. "I summoned a demon."

Quentin's eyes went wide. "A demon, seriously? What did it look like?"

"It looked kind of like a woman... but with green skin and ram horns," Tobey said. He decided not to share the part about his first summoning, where the demon had shown up looking like his dream witch. That seemed private.

"Was she scary?" Quentin had an expression on his face that Tobey couldn't decipher.

"She was... *sexy*, actually," Tobey said in hushed tones, his blue eyes shining.

Quentin broke out in a grin. "I can dig it," he said. "I bet she looked *way* more interesting than any of the girls here at school."

"I was in awe of her," Tobey said. "Such a commanding... presence."

"What did you ask her for?" Quentin said. He'd closed both books and handed Tobey's copy back to him. Tobey slipped it into his backpack.

Tobey's face turned red. He didn't want to talk about being bullied. He held up his left hand, to show Quentin the ring, gleaming black in the cafeteria lights. "This ring gives me... *power*..."

"What kind of power?"

"Power over my enemies," Tobey said solemnly.

Quentin looked skeptical. "Really?"

Tobey looked at him. "Have you seen Charlie Cashbox today?"

The ginger boy looked uneasy. "Yeah, he had a black eye. Somebody really roughed him up."

Tobey smiled like the Cheshire Cat.

Before Quentin could respond, Jessica appeared with a sunny smile on her face. "*There* you are," she said to Quentin, completely ignoring Tobey. Quentin swiftly dumped his copy of the book into his lap before Tobey could even blink. "Don't you want to sit with me and my friends? They're all *really* interested in getting to know you..."

"Uh..." Quentin said, darting a nervous glance at Tobey, who was frowning.

Tobey stood up unexpectedly. Suddenly he was furious at Jessica. His eyes were flashing dangerously. "Leave us alone," he hissed to her, in a deep, menacing voice (with just a touch of a British accent).

Jessica took one step back, her eyes widening in fear... but then she flipped her hair and laughed. "You don't have to be so snippy," she said. "Quentin's my *date* for the dance, and we just wanted to go over some plans."

Tobey looked at Quentin in surprise. Hadn't he said Jessica was a *twat*? Why on earth would he go to the dance with her?

Quentin saw Tobey's puzzled expression and his eyes seemed to turn green. "I'll be right back," he said, and got up from the table.

Tobey watched them walk off—Quentin sliding the book into his backpack without Jessica noticing. The rage he'd felt at Jessica interrupting their private conversation was starting to dissipate... but he still didn't understand. He thought he'd found a friend, but that friend was seemingly dating one of the most obnoxious girls in school.

He sat down, too mystified to continue eating. Pushed his tray aside, he saw there was a piece of paper sticking out from underneath it.

Where did this come from? He unfolded the paper—it was another note from Quentin.

Don't worry, nothing's changed about how I feel about Jessica, the note said. *There are larger things at play here... I'll explain after school.*

Tobey stared at the note, eyes wide. Again he wondered how Quentin had managed to write it and hide it without Tobey seeing. He definitely had powers of his own—that he'd probably gotten from his copy of *Witchcraft*. Although Tobey wasn't sure how he did it, without summoning a demon.

Then he remembered that according to the book, boys could be *witches* in addition to being warlocks or consorts. Witches didn't have to summon demons to do magic. Could Quentin be a witch?

It was the only explanation that sort of made sense.

Jessica took Quentin back to her table where Cara and Lila were sitting.

Lila's eyebrows lifted just a little when she saw them together.

"Guys, this is Quentin Pepper, my date for the dance," she said happily.

"I know," Lila said shortly. "I'm in your homeroom, remember?" She reached out to shake Quentin's hand. "Pleasure to meet you. I'm Lila Fouler, by the way."

"Ah, Lila... you're George Fouler's daughter," Quentin said with a wide, friendly smile.

"That's me," Lila said, flipping her long brown hair over one shoulder. Her expensive jewelry twinkled in the cafeteria lights.

"I really love your style, Lila," Quentin went on. "It's very chic and elegant."

Lila's eyes lit up. "Thank you," she said.

Quentin turned to Cara. "You must be Cara," he said. "That hairstyle suits you perfectly."

"You're so sweet," Cara said, smiling.

Jessica clutched Quentin's arm protectively. So far, her friends *loved* Quentin. But she wanted to make sure they knew he was all hers.

"So, have you shown him your dress yet?" Cara asked Jessica.

"She's told me all about it," Quentin said. "I wanted to coordinate what I'm wearing with what she's wearing, so we'll look perfect together. I heard they'll have a setup for taking photos."

"So thoughtful," Cara said appreciatively. "Most guys, you have to twist their arm to get them interested in clothes, especially formal wear."

"Well, Jessica's a great girl," Quentin said, his hazel eyes shining. "It was the least I could do."

Jessica beamed at him. He was like a fairy-tale prince.

"What kind of car do you drive?" Lila wanted to know.

"Oh, it's my dad's," Quentin said apologetically. Off Lila's disdainful look, he added, "It's a vintage Jaguar XJS. He keeps it in top shape."

Now Lila looked impressed.

"Listen, it was great talking to both of you, but I have a meeting with one of my teachers before my next class," Quentin said, getting up. "See you in French, Jessica."

"Au revoir," Jessica said with a wink. She watched him go, then turned to her friends. "Isn't he the greatest?"

"He almost seems too good to be true," Lila said.

"You're just jealous," Jessica grumbled.

*   *   *

Tobey saw Quentin leave the cafeteria. Where was he going? Hadn't he said he'd be right back? He got up and ran to try to catch up with the new boy.

He spotted Quentin at the end of the hall and ran faster. "Hey! Wait!"

A teacher appeared in a doorway. "No running," she said sternly. "Do you want a detention?"

"No, ma'am," Tobey said. He slowed. The teacher remained in her doorway until Tobey passed. By the time he got to the end of the hallway, Quentin had vanished.

And he was late for gym class. He turned in the opposite direction, heading to the gym.

Everyone else had already changed—including Tom McLay, who kept looking like he was about to ask Tobey something and then changing his mind—so he was in the locker room alone. As Tobey sat to tie his gym sneakers, someone came back into the locker room.

It was Charlie Cashbox. The red of his bruised eye was starting to turn purplish. He scowled at Tobey as he retrieved something from his locker, but he didn't say anything to Tobey. During the class, he ignored Tobey, which was a pleasant change from what had been happening in the last couple of weeks.

But then after class, Charlie shot him a sly look. Was he planning something? Absent-mindedly, Tobey twisted the ring on his finger. He'd kept it on during gym, just in case, and now it was slippery with sweat.

After Charlie left, he took the ring off and put it in his empty right pants pocket—the note from Quentin was in the left one. Just one more class and he'd be able to meet Quentin after school again, he hoped, to continue their conversation.

On a sudden impulse, he pulled the note out and unfolded it.

The writing had changed. Tobey's heart skipped a beat. Now the note read, *Sorry about that. Meet me by my car this time.*

Underneath that, he'd drawn a map of the student parking lot with a star over a particular space.

Tobey glanced around to make sure no one had seen, then left the locker room.

Bruce Fatcat headed to his usual parking spot after school, looking for his black Porsche. When he got to his usual spot, he frowned, remembering from this morning that some jerk who didn't know who Bruce was had parked in his spot. Bruce stalked past the bright-red, 1975 Jaguar convertible and located his car, which was in the row behind it.

As he got in, he noticed a boy approaching the Jaguar. It was Quentin, the new guy. Was that really his car? Bruce didn't know what kind of car he expected the *gay* to drive, but this wasn't it.

He had started the engine, revved it, and was about to peel out of the parking lot when he saw Tobey North walk over. Interesting. Was Tobey also gay? The gangly boy *was* a freak, so it made sense.

He watched as Tobey put his backpack in the space behind the front seat of the passenger's side. Tobey took a small, old-looking book out of the backpack and got in.

Tobey was showing Quentin the book. Bruce couldn't make out what they were saying. He turned the engine off and rolled down his windows.

"Is there anyone else you'd like to get back at?" Quentin was saying. Bruce marveled at how he pitched his voice lower, to hide the fact that he was gay. "Considering what you did to Charlie..."

Bruce frowned. He'd overheard Charlie saying he got into a fight after gym, but he'd boasted that the other guy had it much worse.

"Let's see... Bruce Fatcat," Tobey said. He sounded excited.

Bruce narrowed his eyes. So the weirdo was planning something. He wondered what Quentin would say about him to Tobey, if anything. Thinking about their lunch the other day made Bruce bristle. So far, he'd assumed Quentin had kept mum, because he hadn't heard anything from the other boys he knew.

"With the ring, or are you going to... *call someone up* again?" Quentin asked.

What ring? Bruce had seen Tobey fiddling with something on his left middle finger in the cafeteria. Was that what they were talking about? What could a ring do to his bullies? Maybe it functioned like brass knuckles.

But that was ridiculous. You'd need to have actual strength in your upper arms to be able to hurt someone with one ring on your finger. And Tobey North was a weakling—a tall, stringy, weakling.

"I'm not sure," Tobey mused. "I've got one more *call* I can make... but I don't think it'll work now that the moon is waxing."

What did the moon have to do with anything? Were the two boys talking in some sort of gay code? Annoyed, Bruce started the car again and roared out of the parking lot.

*   *   *

"I need to get home," Tobey said. "My mom hates when I'm late. But I'd really rather stay and talk with you, about the book... Why are there two different copies?"

"I really don't know," Quentin said. "But that's how I learned to communicate with you, with those notes. It's a combination summoning and translocation spell."

"That is so cool," Tobey said. "Can we just communicate that way from now on?"

Quentin shook his head. "Unfortunately, I can only do it two times a day, and even that is pushing it. Using that much magic makes me tired." There was a note of frustration in his voice.

"Too bad," Tobey said, getting out of the Jaguar. He put his copy of *Witchcraft* back in his backpack before pulling it out of the narrow back seat. "But I'll see you in homeroom tomorrow—unless there's traffic, of course."

"And we can still meet after school," Quentin told him. "But not lunch—I have a feeling Jessica will want me to hang around her the whole period, to show me off to her friends."

"Oh, yeah," Tobey said. "You never told me why you agreed to go out with her..."

"It's complicated," Quentin said. "But I can explain more tomorrow. Rest assured, I still think she's an utter twit."

Tobey laughed. "See you tomorrow." He walked over to his car, which was in the far corner of the lot.

His mouth dropped open when he saw someone had slashed his tires.

*   *   *

Tobey's Story

"You're in a good mood," Elizabeth remarked as Jessica got into the Jeep to go home. Her twin was flushed with pleasure and singing to herself.

Jessica checked her reflection in the visor mirror and applied some lip gloss. She laughed. "Didn't I tell you? I have a date for dance! I was a little worried that no hot guy would pop up, but it finally happened, just like it always does—and *boy* was he handsome! I should've realized, the cute ones are always right under my nose!"

Elizabeth started the car and pulled out of the parking space. "Who is he?"

"Quentin Pepper, the new guy," Jessica sighed.

"Quentin?" Elizabeth asked in surprise. "Isn't he —" she stopped, blushing.

"What? Isn't he what?" Jessica demanded.

"Um, nothing," Elizabeth said quickly. She thought about the first time she'd seen Quentin in homeroom—she'd thought he was *gay*. But that couldn't be true if he was taking Jessica to the dance.

I must've been mistaken, she thought as her twin prattled on about the dance, her date, and what they were both going to wear.

*   *   *

Tobey ran back over to the parking space when Quentin's car had been—but the ginger-haired boy had already left. He hadn't even seen him leave.

So much for getting help from my only friend at this school, he thought.

He walked back over to his car to sit in the driver's seat and think. Sure, he could go back inside the school and use the payphone to call a tow truck—*again*—but that seemed unnecessary now that he had a magic book and a magic ring.

He opened the book and flipped through it. There had to be some kind of mending spell... but unlike Quentin's copy, everything in *this* book that looked like a spell required calling up a demon first.

And since it was no longer the new moon, summoning the Nyx again wouldn't work.

He blew out his breath. There had to be something in here... he flipped a few more pages, and stopped when he came to a page he hadn't seen before.

It was a drawing of the ring, under a section entitled "Magical Objects (Given to the Summoner by the Demon)."

"A magic ring usually has one purpose—it gives the wearer a specific power, such as strength, agility, invisibility, or levitation. The wearer can only use it for this one purpose. If he uses it to perform any other spell, he forfeits the former use of the ring thereafter."

The next few pages detailed the types of spells one could use the ring for.

One of them was called "Fix-All Spell."

He bit his lip. So if he used the ring, he could fix his tires, but then he would no longer have the superhuman agility that he'd used to fight off his bullies?

Did he dare? He'd gotten used to the confidence the ring had given him. It had been awesome, going to school knowing that he could fend off any attack.

But now he kind of wanted to see what else the ring could do—even if that meant he couldn't use it again. Maybe Charlie would back off now that Tobey had socked him one.

There are still plenty of other people who have it out for me, he worried.

He glanced down at the page again. If he used the mending spell, it didn't render the ring useless—it changed its purpose.

"The mending spell works for objects and also on minor wounds when directed at the human body."

I could just go inside and use the phone, he told himself. His pants pocket felt warm all of a sudden, and he fished the ring out from inside and slipped it on his finger. It seemed to glow. *It would be cool to see if this works.*

He glanced up at the rearview mirror.

The Nyx was smiling back at him, her yellow eyes gleaming. He inhaled sharply.

"Piper," he breathed.

Tobey's Story

Looks like you need some help in deciding whether to use magic, the Nyx said, her voice echoing in his thoughts.

"Do you think I should do it?" he asked the reflection. "I'll be able to get home, but I won't be able to fight anymore."

But you had so much fun with it, didn't you? Don't you want to see what else it can do?

Besides, you'll see me again come the new moon...

He hesitated. It was true he could summon her again in a few weeks—for the last time. Maybe she'd give him some other magical object that would be even better than the ring.

"OK." He grinned at her, and she faded from the mirror.

Then he got out of the car and looked around. Most of the students had left by now. The rest of the cars belonged to kids who were staying after school.

There was no one around.

He set the book on the top of the trunk, open to the page with the mending spell.

According to the book, he had to twist the ring clockwise three times and say the magic words—they were in Latin again, but the incantation was much shorter than the demon-summoning spell.

He watched as the air around his tires shimmered like on a hot day. The slashes in the rubber knit back together, and the tires re-inflated by themselves.

His face split into a grin. It worked!

Now the ring was cold. *I've changed its purpose,* he told himself.

But he felt incredible. He'd actually worked magic—without first summoning a demon.

He drove home in a state of euphoria.

But he came down a little when he realized he'd lost Quentin's number again. He checked all his pockets. Where had it gone?

*   *   *

"Thanks for the ride home," Tom said as Quentin pulled his Jaguar into the McLays' driveway late that afternoon.

"No problem," Quentin said, smiling at the blonde boy. "I'm sorry for making you wait until everyone was gone." After Tobey had left, he'd pulled his car around the side entrance to pick Tom up.

"It's OK," Tom said. "I get it. You don't want anybody to know you're gay—and neither do I, really. When I realized who I was, I did have a few private conversations about it with people I trusted, but I don't want it broadcast all over school, you know?"

"Absolutely," Quentin said.

"Do you want to come in for a bit? My parents aren't home yet... Or we could have a tennis match in the backyard." His eyes twinkled.

Quentin touched his hand, gazing into Tom's eyes. "That sounds great, but I'll have to take a raincheck. I have some errands to run."

Tom flushed, then nodded. "See you tomorrow." He got out of the passenger's side and walked up to his front door, turning to wave at his new *friend* as he pulled out of the driveway.

*   *   *

That night, while his mother was working late at the nursery, Tobey went all over the house, fixing things with his ring. He repaired his mother's hairdryer, a cracked windowpane in the downstairs bathroom, a rip in the upholstery of one of the living room chairs, and the lawnmower, which had lain unusable in the garage storage cabinet for several months. Mrs. North had been too busy to get it fixed, and Tobey had been borrowing a neighbor's to cut the grass every weekend.

Satisfied, he started dinner. The ring couldn't cook *for* him, he found out, but it *could* "fix" overcooked rice, reversing the damage. He almost wanted to burn the entree to see if he could fix that, but he was too hungry.

Tobey's Story

Using so much magic—even if it was all the ring's doing—somehow made him exhausted, so he was asleep by the time his mother came home.

Chapter 8

Instead of heading home after dropping Tom off, Quentin drove downtown. He was hoping to find the store that his copy of the book had come from. Maybe the proprietor could help him reach Tobey.

He wondered who the shopkeeper would be—he had a hunch it would be someone familiar.

He pulled into the parking lot, looking up at the storefront—it was a cute little boutique called Seraphina's. He got out of the Jag and walked up to the front door, intending to ask someone where he could find the Book Cellar—but then he saw the sign in the alleyway and the stairs going down.

To his disappointment, the door was locked, and the sign said CLOSED. He peered through the window in the door, but the store was very dark.

Well, of course. That would be too easy, he thought, frowning.

He started back towards the car, then stopped and turned around to look at Seraphina's.

It was open, so he went inside.

The store was bright and cheerful, but all the dresses inside reminded him of Jessica—low-cut necklines, bright colors, miniskirts, and long skirts with slits up the thigh. He knew she'd gotten her dress here, but it seemed odd that *every* item of clothing in here was exactly Jessica's style. Looking at several tags, he also saw that everything was exactly Jessica's size.

"Can I help you?" A salesclerk had appeared—a slim girl with long dark hair, pale skin, and shining black eyes.

Quentin did a double take. "Lydia? What are you doing here?" It certainly *looked* like his friend...

The girl looked uneasy and glanced back at the register, where another salesclerk was ringing up a customer. Quentin suddenly realized her expression was one of fear. He couldn't figure out why until he remembered that he was male. A young woman being approached by an unknown guy, acting like he knew her —Jessica Wastefeld would've been thrilled, but any sane teenage girl would proceed with caution.

Her name badge *did* say "Lydia," but she clearly didn't recognize him.

"I'm sorry, do I know you?" she asked timidly.

Quentin cleared his throat. "Um, sorry, no, I guess I mistook you for someone else. Uh... I was just wondering if you knew when the Book Cellar was opening up again?"

Lydia's expression softened, and her shoulders relaxed. Quentin felt an odd stirring of something deep inside him—a kind of predatory feeling. The salesgirl's guard was down, so that meant he could... *what?* Quentin didn't want to consider it. He took a deep breath, trying to squash down the feeling. If he'd been talking to Jessica or Elizabeth, it would be different. But Lydia was an innocent—and she didn't recognize him.

"Mr. August had a personal emergency. I don't think he'll be back for the rest of the week."

"Oh," Quentin said. "Thanks."

He left the store and went home.

Quentin woke up twenty minutes late on Wednesday. He groped for his alarm clock, but it wasn't there.

"What the—?" He opened his eyes, not knowing where he was for a moment.

Tobey's Story

Then he saw the empty space on his nightstand, where the clock had been the night before.

And the rest of the room, which was different than he was expecting. He groaned.

Touché, Saccharin Valley.

He'd clearly been pushing it yesterday, going to the Book Cellar. Saccharin Valley didn't want him snooping around. It seemed keen on holding on to Tobey, even if Tobey didn't belong.

Quentin would have to pace himself.

He got up and nonchalantly went to the bathroom to wash his face, brush his teeth, and comb his hair. Like your average teenage boy. Although he did put the seat back down after using the toilet.

It was still awfully lonely in this big old house with no parents or cats. He kept hoping to hear the phone ring, but Tobey didn't call. What was he waiting for?

In the shower, he yelped—there was no hot water.

The tires on Tobey's car were still in perfect condition when he got up. He left for school ten minutes early, to try to beat the traffic. He'd had an amazing night's sleep, no dreams.

He really wanted to tell Quentin about what had happened with the ring.

But when he got to homeroom, the new boy wasn't there. Jessica was in the back talking to Lila, and Elizabeth was in the second row, chatting with Enid. She met his gaze as he walked by, then quickly looked down.

He remembered his dream about her and grinned. He was closer than ever to being the evil sorcerer of his dreams. Not that he wanted to sacrifice either Wastefeld twin on his altar—in fact, with his newfound power, he realized he didn't care about them at all.

But then he realized he'd have to talk to Jessica if he wanted to ask where Quentin was. He wondered how much time Quentin and Jessica had spent together outside of school now that they were a couple.

I really need to ask him what's going on, he thought. If Quentin was a witch, maybe he had something interesting planned for Jessica at the dance.

Tobey definitely wanted to know about it if so.

Charlie Cashbox slunk in late, taking a seat in the corner without looking at Tobey. Although he did purposely step on a pencil Tobey had just dropped. It broke into two pieces.

Tobey put the pieces in his desk, smiling to himself. He wanted to try the mending spell again, but not while there were so many other people around.

He glanced back at Jessica. She and Lila were still deep in conversation. The bell was about to ring.

Then the door opened—and Quentin strode through it, looking flushed. His hair was still wet from the shower. He was wearing another Henley shirt, khakis, and boots.

"You're late, Mr. Pepper," the homeroom teacher admonished. She marked him in her attendance book, and then the bell rang.

Tobey shot up from his desk to follow Quentin as he turned around and left the classroom. "Hey, Quentin," he called. Quentin kept walking, but Tobey caught up with him at his locker.

"Where were you this morning?" he asked.

"I overslept," Quentin grumbled, grabbing books out of his locker. He seemed to be in a hurry.

"I wanted to ask you—"

"No time," Quentin said. "Sorry, Tobey. I've got to get to my first class." He touched Tobey on the shoulder, and then slammed his locker door shut. Before Tobey could respond, he'd disappeared into the crowded hallway.

The morning seemed to stretch out indefinitely. Tobey spent most of his first four classes alternately looking at the clock, wondering if he'd be able to catch Quentin in the halls, and paging through his notebooks, in case the witch boy had magicked him another note.

So far, there was nothing.

He began to doodle in the margins of one page of notes—drawing an evil sorcerer with a skullcap, goatee, and long robes.

Tobey's Story

When lunchtime finally came around, he hurried down the hall, but he saw Olivia standing by her locker, and her eyes lit up when she saw him.

"Hey, Tobey," she said.

Tobey wanted to keep walking, but something made him stop and smile back at her. *I really shouldn't be encouraging her,* he thought.

"I just wanted to let you know, I asked Elizabeth if we could print one of your drawings in the *Oracle*," she said.

He blinked in surprise. He'd expected her to ask about the dance.

"Oh," he said. "OK. Sure, I'll see what I can find."

He hurried away from her, bumping into Bruce as he left the bathroom. "Watch it," Bruce cried.

"Sorry," Tobey mumbled. He tried to move past Bruce, but the older boy blocked his way.

Bruce looked him up and down with a smirk. "*Love* the threads," he said sarcastically.

Tobey was wearing a blue dress shirt, baggy trousers, suspenders, and wing-tip shoes.

"Who does your tailoring? Guys and Dolls?" Bruce sneered.

"Sod off," Tobey growled, the British accent coming out again.

Bruce barked a short laugh, which died in his throat as he looked into Tobey's eyes. All the color drained from his face.

Tobey could feel his eyes prickling with that power again. He smiled his creepiest smile. "See you around," he said pleasantly, then pushed Bruce aside and kept walking.

He felt Bruce's scowl on his back as he left. But he didn't care—he'd survived an interaction with one of his bullies without needing the ring's former power. *I could get used to this,* he thought.

Even though he might be late for class, he ducked into the bathroom to try the mending spell on the broken pencil.

He twisted the ring, spoke the words, and the two pieces leapt toward each other as if magnetized, the rough wood ends melding together seamlessly. The newly mended pencil shimmered in the bathroom lights.

Excellent, he thought. He wondered what other things he could do at school, with this spell.

At lunch, Quentin was sitting with Todd, Aaron, and Winston. Tobey walked right by their table, raising an eyebrow at Quentin.

He went to sit at his usual table in the corner. Maybe Quentin would come over later. He'd said there were spies everywhere, so maybe sitting with the popular boys was some pretense he felt he had to keep up.

Once Tobey sat down, he opened his lunch box and started pulling the smaller containers out of it. He'd brought sashimi and tempura this time.

There was no note in there.

Hmm, I wonder, he thought, and pulled the *Witchcraft* book out of his bag.

A small piece of paper fluttered out as he opened it. Tobey's heartbeat sped up. He unfolded it.

Can't talk now, it said in Quentin's oddly feminine handwriting. *Got to keep up appearances. But about Jessica—I promise you, taking her to the dance is all part of a grand plan than I have.*

Which involves a certain book.

His eyes widened. How did Quentin know what he was going to ask him? Was "mind-reading" one of the spells in his copy of *Witchcraft*? He hadn't seen *that* in the contents.

As he stared at the words, they slowly disappeared and were replaced with new ones.

Meet me in the library after school if you want to talk.

Looking across the room, he saw Quentin looking at him, his hazel eyes glowing green like the eyes of the witch from his dreams. The boy tilted his head slightly, as if communicating a question.

Tobey nodded, slowly and deliberately, then went back to his lunch.

Tobey's Story

*   *   *

Tom couldn't wait to see Quentin in Chemistry. They were paired up as lab partners again, to his delight. Quentin *had* to be the one. They'd gotten to talking on the ride home the previous day, and as it turned out, Quentin didn't play tennis, but he was willing to learn. And he liked the same kind of books that Tom liked: science fiction.

Quentin looked troubled today. Tom ached for his new friend to confide in him.

Maybe if Tom asked him to the dance, that would cheer him up.

But Mr. Russo was watching them like a hawk while they did their experiments. Tom thought about writing Quentin a secret note.

Then something incredibly lucky happened—Mr. Russo was called down to the office briefly. "I'll be back in a few minutes," he said sternly. "Please keep working quietly."

"Hey, uh, Quentin," Tom said in a low voice once the teacher had gone. As soon as he'd gone, the students started talking to each other loudly, ignoring the teacher's direction. "Are you going to the dance on Friday?"

Quentin's eyes gleamed green behind his safety goggles. "I was thinking about it," he said slowly.

"I mean, I saw you hanging around Jessica and her friends at lunch. I thought you might be going with one of them..."

Quentin reddened slightly. "So, well, I actually told Jessica I was going with her... but I don't really *like* her."

"So why are you going with her, then?"

Quentin took a deep breath. "Jessica is... my beard."

"Beard?" Tom echoed. "What does that mean?"

"Oh, you *are* new to this," Quentin said with a small smile.

Tom huffed, not sure if he should be insulted.

Quentin touched him on the arm. "It's OK... You don't want anyone to know you're gay, right? 'Beard'

101

means I'm taking Jessica so everyone will think I'm straight."

"Oh," Tom said, thinking hard. "So you don't have any romantic feelings for Jessica?"

Quentin laughed shortly. "Far from it," he said. "I only have eyes for you, babe." His hazel eyes twinkled.

Tom smiled. "Well, if Jessica's your fake date, would you like a *real* date? Even if it's a secret? Would you like to go with"—here Tom looked around to make sure no one was eavesdropping—"*me?*" The last word was spoken in the faintest whisper, while he pointed to his own chest, just to be clear.

Quentin grinned at him. "I'd love to."

Leaving class that day, Tom felt as if he'd been filled with helium.

Tobey found Quentin in a carrel in the study area of the library. The broad-shouldered boy looked up at him and smiled. He'd been leafing through his copy of *Witchcraft*. As soon as Tobey sat down, he said in a whisper, "Tell me more about the ring the demon gave you."

Tobey's eyes lit up. "Well, it *had* given me a kind of super-strength—or agility—but then I changed its purpose with a spell."

Quentin furrowed his brow. "Changed its purpose? I didn't know you could do that..."

Tobey glanced around to make sure there was no one in their corner of the library before replying in a low voice. "You're not a warlock or a sorcerer, are you? You're a... *witch.*"

Quentin's eyes widened, looking green again instead of hazel. "Yes, that's right. I guess that's why my copy of the book doesn't have anything about demons..."

He gestured towards his copy, flipping back to the table of contents. Tobey thought he'd remembered seeing some loose pages stuffed into the back of the book, but they weren't there now. Maybe Quentin had gotten Mr. August to glue them back in properly.

"Yeah, I noticed that," Tobey said, pulling out his own copy. "But mine *does* have demons. In fact, there's nothing I can really do without summoning a demon first. And there's only one demon in here—the Nyx."

He showed Quentin the page with the rendering of the demon, but the boy didn't seem interested. "But you got the ring from her, right? So how did you change what it was for?"

Tobey turned to the page about objects obtained from summoned demons. "I just did this spell. Yesterday, after I left you, I saw that someone had slashed my tires..."

"Oh, no," Quentin said. "I'm so sorry. I had to leave shortly after you, otherwise I could've helped."

"It was no big deal," Tobey said with a sly grin. "That's where this spell comes in. I used it on the ring, and then the ring on my tires. I changed its purpose to 'mending.'"

"You're kidding," Quentin said, looking at him. "You could have just called a tow truck..."

"Yeah, well, I'd already done that last week," Tobey grumbled. "Besides, look what I can do now." He picked up a cast-off library book that someone had left in the carrel and ripped out a page.

"Don't!" Quentin hissed. "The librarian will hear you!"

Tobey briefly wondered when Quentin had gotten so uptight about magic. Or maybe he just didn't like seeing books destroyed? "I think she's gone for the day. Watch." He twisted the ring and said the words. Then he held the page up to the book—immediately it got pulled back into the binding and the torn edges melded back together.

He thought Quentin would be impressed, but the ginger-haired boy was scowling. "You gave up super strength for *bookbinding?*" He seemed annoyed.

Tobey faltered. What was wrong with his new friend? He seemed like he was in a bad mood. "Well, I was also able to fix a lot of broken stuff around the house... *and* it works on minor wounds."

"But that's *healing* magic, not preventative," Quentin argued. "I just don't understand why you'd do that. The demon gave you an incredible gift, and you just..." He left off, seemingly too frustrated to continue.

Tobey shifted uncomfortably in his plastic chair. "Well, I'm still using it. Besides, she *wanted* me to try that spell."

"She did?" Quentin looked alarmed now.

Tobey nodded. "I could see her in the rearview mirror, looking pleased."

"Oh," Quentin said softly. "Well, can you change it back?"

"No, I can't change the power of the ring to what it once was... maybe I could change it to something *else*, though," Tobey said. "It's not a huge deal. My bullies are quiet all of a sudden."

Quentin was silent, deep in thought.

"Anyway, what kinds of things can you do as a witch? I've never heard of a boy witch... I mean, not until I read that book."

Quentin stared at him for a moment, as if deciding whether to engage with the change of subject. "Well, I told you about my sixth sense," Quentin said. "It's what led me to you."

"Really?" Tobey said in surprise.

Quentin put his hand on Tobey's knee. "Yeah," he said softly. "When I saw you, I just knew we'd known each other in a past life."

Tobey jerked away as Quentin's hand slid up his thigh. "What are you doing?"

Quentin yanked his hand away. "Sorry," he said. Tobey felt his face turning red, but the other boy didn't seem embarrassed by what he'd just done.

Quentin glanced at his watch. "Oh, I have to go." He picked up his dark green backpack, stuffed his *Witchcraft* book into it, and got up.

"Wait," Tobey said. "I want to know more about witch magic."

"Tomorrow," Quentin said over his shoulder as he walked away.

Tobey wanted to get up and run after him, but he was frozen in place. Something was holding him in the chair! It was like a force field, preventing him from getting up.

As he watched Quentin leave the library, part of him wondered if this was a spell that Quentin had cast

Tobey's Story

on him. Why would he do that? Why was Quentin so mysterious? Every conversation he'd had with Quentin left him with more questions than answers.

Then Tobey realized he'd better get on home. He wondered how long the spell transfixing him would last. Just as Quentin exited through the library doors, he could move again. He shot up and ran out of the library, trying to catch up with Quentin yet again—but the boy was gone.

And I forgot to get his number again. It would've been kind of embarrassing to ask for a third time, anyway, he thought.

Dejected, Tobey plodded to his locker to put his books away. He threw them inside with no regard for what they were and which ones he needed for homework. Suddenly he just wanted to go home and lie down. His jacket caught on the edge of the locker door and he yanked on it, hearing a faint *ping*. Thinking it was his zipper pull hitting the metal locker door, he grabbed his nearly-empty backpack, shut the door, and left the school, heading for his car.

*   *   *

Quentin drove home from the school, biting his full, unadorned lower lip (well, he'd used some ChapStick, that was it). What Tobey had told him about the ring was worrisome. And the demon in Tobey's rearview mirror... *that* Nyx hadn't been him.

What was happening?

Maybe Saccharin Valley was trying to undo the damage he'd done by forcing it to accommodate demon summoning (and his presence). He could feel the sunny, fictional town pushing back against him being here. It had already turned him into a boy. What else could it do?

He'd have to tread carefully if he wanted to help Tobey.

Chapter 9

"You're late again," Tobey's mom pointed out when he got home.

"I'm sorry," he said, putting his jacket away in the hall closet. "I had to go to the school library after classes let out... to get some books for a project." He shifted his very light backpack, hoping she wouldn't notice the lack of books.

"Well, I've put dinner in the oven, so could you take over? I have some packing to do, for another business trip."

Tobey had already started toward the kitchen, but he stopped when she said this and turned around. "Again? But you just got back, two days ago."

"That was for the nursery," Mrs. North explained. "This is for the boutique."

"Oh," Tobey said, staring at her. His mother had always been busy, but never *this* busy. He supposed it was fine—if she was gone, there'd be less chance she would find out what he was doing with his father's things... and with Quentin, at school.

He went to set the table, thinking about Quentin and his witch magic... and his hand on Tobey's knee.

He realized he wasn't as put off as the other boys at school would've been. In fact, now that he thought about it, it seemed kind of... *nice*. He flushed, remembering.

Now he was confused. He'd thought he liked strictly girls—or at least, red-haired witches. Did he also like boys too?

And if so, what did that make him?

There had to be a word for it, but he racked his mind and came up empty.

The oven timer went off, and all thoughts of labelling his sexuality went out of his head as he donned two oven mitts and pulled the pan out of the oven. It needed a few more minutes, he decided, so he slid it back in.

His mother came back down when dinner was ready, and they ate in comfortable silence until Mrs. North spoke up. "I noticed my hair dryer works perfectly now. Isn't that funny? It had been giving me so much trouble—sometimes I'd plug it in and it wouldn't even turn on!"

Oops, Tobey thought. He shouldn't have been so gung-ho about using the ring. He wondered if she'd noticed any of the other fixes he'd made.

Hastily, he took a drink of his water. "I guess sometimes things just... fix themselves?" he said.

"I suppose that could happen," Mrs. North said, a pensive look on her face. "Well, anyway... Have you made a new friend at school, Tobias?"

Tobey paused with a forkful of chicken parmesan halfway to his mouth. "A new friend? Erm, no," he managed. "Why do you ask?"

"It's just that since I've been back, I've noticed you seem a little... happier, lately." She had put her napkin down and was resting her chin on one elegant hand, looking at him with the oddest expression on her face.

Tobey couldn't help but be nervous as he avoided his mother's large, lavender-blue eyes, picking at his own napkin. Did she know what was going on? No... she couldn't. She'd been so busy with the nursery since she'd gotten back—she'd said there'd been a large shipment of exotic plants she'd had to bring back from up north, that was what the first trip had been for. She'd come home late almost every night and left early each morning, so they'd barely seen each other.

"Oh, it must be because I found a... *creative solution* to dealing with my bullies," he said carefully. His mother was well aware of the bullying situation and had always advised him to tell a teacher, but he'd never taken her advice, knowing that doing so only would lead to more trouble.

"Really?" Mrs. North said, taking a sip of her elderberry wine. "That's wonderful! How did you manage that?"

Tobey took a deep breath, trying to stall for time, but the phone rang. Mrs. North jumped up to answer it. It was a work call, and she took it in the small downstairs bedroom she used as a study.

Once she was gone, Tobey hurriedly finished his food, cleared his place, and went upstairs to do homework.

Right before bed, his mother knocked on his bedroom door. "I just wanted to say goodbye," she said. "Since I'll be gone before you wake up tomorrow."

Tobey smiled at her, and she hugged him and gave him a kiss on the cheek.

"Hard at work on that project, I see," Mrs. North said, beaming. "It makes me so proud to see you staying on top of things."

She turned to leave, but paused at the door. "Oh, before I forget, I found this on the floor in the front hall closet. Who's Quentin?"

Tobey looked at her with alarm. She was holding a scrap of paper that he recognized: Quentin's phone number, which he thought he'd lost (for the second time). It must've fallen out of his jacket.

He snatched the paper from her. "Erm, he's my study partner for this project," he said, thinking, again, that it was better to include some truth in his lie. "I was meeting him at the library today."

"Oh, well, that's wonderful," Mrs. North said. "Is he a nice fellow? Someone you could be... *friends* with?"

Tobey didn't like the odd inflection she gave to that one word. "Yeah, I mean, I guess," he said. "We've only just started, so I don't know him that well."

Mrs. North nodded, but there was that strange look in her eyes again. "Well, have a good day at school tomorrow. I'll be back late Friday evening."

"I will," Tobey said, relieved that she wasn't asking him about the dance. He definitely didn't have a date, but he wasn't interested in going, anyway.

Not unless the Nyx could be his date.

He lay back on his pillow, letting his mind wander. He began to imagine this scenario: showing up to the "Lucky" dance in a vintage burnt-orange suit, a four-leafed clover in his lapel, with a tall, horned demon on his arm. Maybe she'd have a tiny Venus flytrap for a corsage. He smiled to himself, and then the mental image changed. It wasn't the Nyx on his arm. Now it was Quentin, dressed in a long black robe with green trim. The ginger-haired boy shot him a grin in his mind's eye, and his eyes glowed green.

Tobey's eyes flew open. He hadn't meant to think about Quentin like that. His heart fluttered, and he tried to focus on his schoolwork.

Once his mother had gone to bed, he crept out into the hall to use the telephone. It was cordless, so he brought the receiver into his bedroom and closed the door.

With bated breath, Tobey dialed Quentin's number. Now that he could talk to him outside of school, he was eager to ask his new friend all the questions he had about witch magic.

His heart thudded in his chest as he listened to the rings on the other end. One, two, three... he frowned.

After eight rings, he hung up. Maybe Quentin had already gone to bed.

Well, I'll try to catch him at school tomorrow.

That night, Quentin was taking no chances—he'd found another alarm clock in what he supposed was his parents' room (the beds hadn't been slept in), and put it on his bedside table. His own alarm clock was still mysteriously missing. He'd set this new one for an hour early, just in case.

In Saccharin Valley, he slept deeply, without dreams.

But when he woke, it wasn't because the alarm had gone off. It was because the room was unusually dark. He'd left the curtains open, so if all else failed, he'd wake up to the sunlight streaming through the window.

There was no sunlight this morning. Then what had woken him up? He sat up and rubbed his eyes blearily.

The sunlight was completely blocked, and he had to turn on a lamp to see what was going on. When he looked across the room at the window, he blinked in confusion.

The window seemed to be covered in tightly-knit green vines. He got up and ran over to it, trying to pull it open. It was stuck at first, and then with a mighty groan, it slid upwards.

The vines were thorny, and once the window was open, they pressed in, blocking any way out. He tried to break them apart but got pricked with a thorn. "Ow," he muttered, sucking the drop of blood from his finger.

This was too weird.

He pulled the *Witchcraft* book out from under his mattress and paged through it. There was the spell for communicating with animals—but there was nothing about influencing plants. And there were the torn-out pages for summoning the Hellcniht, which hadn't worked. He'd left them at home when he'd shown Tobey his book again at the library the day before—he didn't want Tobey getting any more ideas about summoning demons.

Quentin frantically flipped pages. The last chapter was something he hadn't noticed before—it seemed to be text from a fairy tale, *Sleeping Beauty*.

What was this doing here? Was it filler? Maybe it was a clue to rescuing Tobey...

And then he heard faint voices downstairs.
Who's there?

Carefully he made his way down the narrow stairs to the second floor.

SACCHARIN VALLEY HIGH

Yes, there was definitely someone downstairs. He wondered how he'd been able to hear them from all the way in the tower room. Maybe it was clairaudience, another spell he'd used from the book.

He stood at the top of the back staircase that led from the second floor to the kitchen, and opened his third eye.

There were two adults down there, sitting at the small table in the breakfast nook and talking. Somehow Quentin couldn't make out their words; it was as if they were underwater. Back home, that would mean that they'd cast an anti-eavesdropping spell.

That sort of thing didn't usually happen in Saccharin Valley.

Then again, Tobey did *cast a spell to summon me as the Nyx.*

The most surprising thing about the couple was that they both looked *very* familiar.

He ran down the stairs.

They turned when they saw him, no expressions on their faces. Quentin couldn't believe his eyes.

The man and woman looked *exactly* like Tobey's parents back in the Witch World.

"August?" Quentin said incredulously. "And Maeve? What are you two doing here? Are you trying to save Tobey too?"

"That's *Mr.* August, young man," said the man. "I don't believe we've made your acquaintance..."

"Because I'm not a young man, usually," Quentin said.

They both looked at him in confusion, and he realized he probably wouldn't be able to explain further without his scene being cut short. He could feel Jessica Wastefeld waiting in the wings, ready to come on at a moment's notice, to take the reader's attention away from him.

"You certainly *look* like a young man," the woman who looked like Tobey's mum remarked, stepping closer and examining him. "And from what the ficus in the hall confirmed for me, *you're* the young man who we've been instructed to keep away from our son."

Tobey's Story

This was interesting. Quentin wondered if that had anything to do with the vines covering the tower room window. Back in the Witch World, Maeve was part Fae, and she could influence plants to grow—or shrivel—at her whim, and communicate with them.

"You've been instructed? By whom?" Quentin wanted to know. "Also, the *ficus* told you? No fair, *you* get to keep your powers here?" An annoyed scowl crossed his handsome face. "All I got was a gender swap, and some piddling psychic abilities."

Maeve's large blue eyes turned cold. "That's none of your concern, *Quentin*," she said.

"I'm not Quentin, I'm Piper," Quentin said. "You know, your son is my consort back where we're from?"

"*Consort?*" growled August. "My son is no such thing."

"And what do you mean, *back where we're from?*" Maeve added. "Both of us have lived in Saccharin Valley our whole lives."

"No, you haven't," Quentin argued. "You're either simulacra, or you're under a spell." *Careful*, he told himself. If he tried to argue with these people any more, Saccharin Valley would likely yank the scene out from under him like a rug.

"He's going to be a handful, certainly," Maeve murmured to her husband. "Have you warded the doors?"

Quentin wasn't listening—he could feel his sixth sense prickling with danger. Something was very, very wrong here. He glanced at the clock over the stove—it was already time to leave for school. "Shit," he muttered. (At this, thunder rumbled outside, as if the narrator was mad at him for swearing.)

"Be careful what you say, dearie," August said softly, his dark eyes gleaming.

Quentin ignored this. He was still in his pajamas, but he had to go. The sense of danger was now a sense of urgency—he *had* to get out of here and find Tobey. With a quick glance at both Tobey's parents, he bolted for the back door.

They made no move to stop him, and he soon saw why.

When he yanked open the door and tried to exit, it was like slamming into a wall. "Ow," he muttered. Something sucked him back into the kitchen, and the door shut itself in front of him.

"We would prefer it if you stayed," August said with a menacing look on his face. He waved a hand, and Quentin was pulled into one of the chairs and forced to sit.

This can't be good.

When Tobey got to school, he saw that Quentin was absent. *Maybe he's just late,* he thought. There hadn't been any traffic that morning, at least not for Tobey. But he didn't know where Quentin lived, so he supposed the boy could be coming from a different area of town.

In homeroom, something seemed off. Charlie wasn't there, and both Wastefeld twins seemed interested in him. Elizabeth wanted to talk to him about publishing some of his drawings in the *Oracle,* and while they were talking, Jessica sidled up to them. "Hey, Liz. Hi, Tobey," she said brightly, as if all the previous snubs of him were water under the bridge. "Have either of you seen Quentin this morning? He's taking me to the dance."

Tobey stared at the friendly look on Jessica's face for a moment, then said flatly, "No, I haven't seen him."

"Oh, OK," Jessica said, tossing her hair. "Well, if you see him later, can you tell him I want to talk to him?"

"Sure," Tobey grunted. In the back of his mind, alarm bells were going off.

Had something happened to Quentin?

Jessica flounced off, and Elizabeth's forehead wrinkled with concern. "I hope Quentin's OK," she said.

Tobey arched one eyebrow. What did Elizabeth care about the new boy? Then he remembered that Elizabeth was nice to everybody.

"You two are friends, right? I've seen you sitting together at lunch," Elizabeth went on.

Tobey's Story

"That's right," Tobey said guardedly. He suddenly felt like Elizabeth was making an *assumption* about him... something that he didn't have a problem with, but his bullies definitely did.

Just then the bell rang, and Tobey blew out his breath in relief. "Gotta go," he said, standing up from his chair.

"If you find some of the drawings you mentioned, you can bring them to the *Oracle* office at lunch," Elizabeth said.

But Tobey had already left.

Quentin sat on one side of the kitchen table, and Tobey's parents—or whoever they were—sat on the other side.

They both had steaming mugs of tea. August, or his imposter, saw Quentin noticing this and silently got up to fetch the kettle from the stove and pour Quentin some in a blue mug with a moon's face on it.

Quentin didn't touch the beverage. In the Fae Realm, if you ate or drank anything while you were there, you'd never be able to leave. Quentin didn't put it past either of them to try to keep him here with a trick like that. Even with the vines and the wards.

He ran his tongue over the back of his teeth. His mouth was very dry.

With his third eye, he could see the wards shimmering over the windows and door. At least there was some light in here—though the sky was getting dark outside, it wasn't as dark as in his bedroom up on the third floor. Maeve must've used her magic to block only the upper floors' windows, while August used his sorcery to make the lower floor exits impenetrable.

"So," Quentin said through gritted teeth. What was the use of being in this hulking *male* form if he couldn't use it to intimidate people? He'd certainly intimidated the sales clerk at Seraphina's. He drummed his thick, manly fingers on the table. "You say I can't see Tobey. For how long?"

"As long as it takes," Maeve said crisply. "But, until after the dance would be a good start..."

"You don't want me at the biggest dance of this here book—I mean, of the whole school year?" Quentin asked. "Why? *Tobey* isn't going... I, on the other hand, have *two* hot dates." He smirked at both of them.

Maeve looked horrified at this information, putting her hand on her heart. "*Two* dates? How tacky."

"Unheard of," August huffed.

"Slut," Maeve added.

Quentin burst out laughing. They couldn't be serious. This was a doozy of a spell Tobey's parents were under.

"We were told you were... *queer*," August added, the last word hissing out through his bared teeth. "And we're not allowing such an influence on our son."

Queer, Quentin thought, blowing out his breath in annoyance. Saccharin Valley didn't know the meaning of the word; he was sure of it.

He stared at Tobey's father. He didn't remember Tobey saying anything about having a father in Saccharin Valley. Back in the Witch World, of course, Tobey had two parents (who didn't care who Tobey dated, as long as he was happy).

This fellow certainly *looked* like Tobey's father. But there was something different about him. Quentin wasn't sure what.

He gazed into the bottom of the mug August had placed in front of him. He thought he could see sparkles in the bottom, like light dancing on the ocean floor.

That definitely does not look right, he thought.

"Can I at least get dressed?" Quentin asked at last, with a winning smile. "I feel silly sitting here in my pajamas."

Tobey's parents exchanged glances. They seemed to be communicating without words. Finally, August nodded. "Go ahead," he said. "But don't expect to find any way *out* up there."

"The phone line is down, too," Maeve added.

"Yes, I figured," Quentin huffed, and dashed up the back stairs.

He checked every window he passed on the way to his room, but they were all covered in thorny vines, just as they had been on the way down.

Tobey's Story

*   *   *

In all his morning classes, the attitudes of all the students who were acquainted with Tobey had shifted slightly—they still mostly avoided him, but there was no more bullying. *Maybe a taste of my ring scared them off,* he thought in his first-period class.

Then he realized his finger felt naked. He looked down.

The ring was gone.

His stomach plummeted. *Oh no.*

He tried to stay calm, to breathe. But panic was creeping in. The one thing the demon had given him, that had changed his life so dramatically, and he'd lost it! He checked his pockets and rummaged through his backpack. No ring. Had it fallen off? But he would've felt it if it had, right?

When class was done, he bolted out the door to search his locker.

There was no sign of it.

It's OK, he tried to tell himself. *I'm still a warlock. I can summon demons.*

Well, one *demon.*

...During the new moon.

And then he remembered the day before, when Bruce had taunted him—the ring had been for mending, not power, then, and he'd done just fine.

He blew out his breath slowly.

He tried to summon that confidence again—and felt the prickling behind his eyes.

I am Tobias Harlan O'Connell Riordan North— son of a great sorcerer.

The ring was gone, but maybe the power had been inside him all along.

Quentin showered and dressed, in a red shirt, black jeans, thick-soled black boots, and a long black duster. Not his usual style, but he was feeling defiant.

He'd also sent a message to Tobey. It took all of his energy to cast the spell, and he worried that the vines growing over the outer windows would prevent it from going through, just as they prevented phone calls from going out. Several attempts at writing the truth resulted in the note fizzling out into nothing. But then, in one frantic final attempt, he wrote something cryptic, like all his earlier notes to Tobey, and mercifully, he could feel it being sent. (There was a little *whoosh* noise in his mind, like how an outgoing email would sound in the future.)

He didn't have high hopes that Tobey could read between the lines, though.

Quentin's eyes widened as he returned to the kitchen and saw that the table was now piled with breakfast food—scrambled eggs, bacon, buttermilk biscuits, pancakes, and fresh fruit.

"We thought it only fair to feed you if we're going to keep you prisoner here," Maeve said, with a sunny smile.

Quentin spied a plate of chocolate crêpes with fresh raspberries, and his stomach rumbled. This was going to be harder than he thought.

Tobey didn't have much time to think any more about the missing ring, as the atmosphere in his next class was also different. The teacher had somehow gained a new interest in him. It was art class, and Mr. James wanted him to show the class his drawing techniques. Helplessly, he complied, taking care not to draw any of the things he'd been drawing recently. No witches, evil sorcerers, or busty twins in Medieval armor.

When he left, he had a folder of one-panel line-drawing cartoons done in pen and ink that would be perfect for the school newspaper.

He wasn't quite sure how *that* had happened.

Not that I'll be seeking out Elizabeth again, he thought. Figuring out what had happened to Quentin was his first priority. Elizabeth, like her sister, would have to learn that everything didn't always go her way.

"I'm not hungry," Quentin said, stalling for time.

Tobey's Story

"Eat," growled August in a menacing voice. "You may be queer, but I'm sure you have as good an appetite as any *normal* boy."

A snarl escaped Quentin's lips. *I'm getting tired of these slurs,* he thought. It was weird hearing such words come out of August's usually pleasant face. (It wasn't the word so much as the *tone*—in the Witch World, queerness was celebrated.)

Quentin closed his eyes, thinking about the book upstairs. How the last chapter was not a spell, but text from a fairy tale.

He remembered the evil fairy turning into a fire-breathing dragon.

I don't have nearly enough power to do anything like that, he thought.

...Do I?

Then he remembered that the evil fairy had made thorny vines grow over the castle, before turning into a dragon.

Maybe he could make them *shrink* instead of growing.

His gaze strayed to the kitchen windowsill, where a potted plant had been placed. It was *mentha piperita*—his namesake. Or rather, *Piper's* namesake.

Or maybe...

Chapter 10

In Spanish, the teacher had Tobey read his essay out loud, and go over pronunciation with the students who were having trouble. When it was finally time for lunch, he hurried along to the cafeteria, hoping that he'd find Quentin there. But instead, Mr. Collins flagged him down.

"Tobey, there you are," he said warmly. "Olivia and Elizabeth have been raving about your drawings. I was hoping you'd consent to eating your lunch here in the *Oracle* office today, and we can look through them together?"

Tobey's heart sank. *Just tell him no,* he thought. *Be polite, but firm. You don't have time, but maybe another day.*

But then Elizabeth and Olivia appeared behind Mr. Collins, along with the paper's photographer, Allen Falters. They all surrounded him and gave him identical friendly smiles.

"We thought we could run some in the very next issue," Elizabeth said.

"With a byline," Olivia assured him, misinterpreting his hesitation.

"What do you say?" Mr. Collins asked, beaming. "It looks like you've brought your lunch, so you're all set.

There's a soda machine in the teacher's lounge, and I can grab you something for you if you'd like."

Tobey sighed inwardly. "Sure," he said finally.

He could always catch up with Quentin after school.

* * *

In the cafeteria, Jessica was eating lunch with Lila and Cara.

"Where's your new boyfriend?" Lila wanted to know. "You've been practically attached at the hip these last few days."

"Oh, he's feeling a little under the weather," Jessica fibbed. She hadn't seen Tobey since homeroom, and even though he was a creep, he was the one person who could find out where Quentin was.

She was starting to worry.

"Well, I hope he isn't too sick to take you to the dance tomorrow night. That would be a bummer," Lila said.

Seeing the gleam in Lila's eye, Jessica felt a twinge of annoyance. She thought fast. "Actually, don't tell anyone, but he called me on the payphone this morning after homeroom," she invented. "He said he's playing hooky so he can find the *perfect* clothes to wear to the dance... and he's picking up a special corsage for me, of course."

"He's so wonderful," Cara gushed.

"A little too wonderful," Lila murmured. "Well, Rowan has been calling me every night, and he speaks fluent French. It's *so* romantic."

Jessica stabbed a fork into her salad. "Quentin's getting his car washed, waxed, and detailed too," she said. This was something he'd actually told her. "I can't wait for tomorrow night."

* * *

Quentin had just finished a pile of chocolate crêpes. They'd been heavenly. He was stalling for time.

Tobey's Story

While he chowed down, Maeve and August—or Mr. August, whoever—were watching him like a hawk.

"There now, don't you feel better?" Maeve cooed. "Isn't it nice to have a day off from school? Such drudgery..."

"Oh, sure," Quentin said sarcastically. "Being held prisoner is the perfect day off."

"There's no need to be rude," Maeve sniffed. She looked to her husband. "August, don't you have something to attend to in the parlor?"

August looked at her, grunted, and got up from the table. Quentin watched him leave with a feeling of dread in the pit of his (very full) stomach.

"What are you doing?" he asked Maeve. "It isn't enough to have prevented my escape?"

"Don't worry your handsome little head about it," Maeve said. "In fact, why don't you take a *nap*?" She shot him a savage grin.

Quentin's stomach gave a weird little gurgle, and he started to feel woozy.

Maeve's smiling face multiplied and swam in his vision. "There, now," she said, but her voice sounded far away.

I knew I shouldn't have eaten anything, he thought, before blacking out.

*   *   *

Tobey listlessly handed over the folder of cartoons he'd produced in art class that morning. He didn't care whether his drawings were published in the paper. He only wanted to make sure Quentin was OK. He glanced up at the clock on the wall. It seemed to be ticking slower than it was supposed to. He groaned inwardly. This was agony.

He picked at his lunch while Mr. Collins looked at the cartoons, chuckling as he read each caption. "These are really funny, Tobey," he said, clapping Tobey on the shoulder. "I had no idea you were so talented."

"Thank you," Tobey said stiffly. He caught Elizabeth looking at him with concern and stared back, trying to summon that prickling in his eyes that would make her back off, as he'd done to Bruce. It must've succeeded, because her face paled and she jumped up from the table.

"I l-left something in my locker," she stammered, and dashed out the door.

Mr. Collins looked up from the paper in his hands with mild surprise, but then Olivia handed him another drawing. "I think *this* one would fit perfectly with the theme of our next issue," she gushed.

Tobey wasn't listening. He felt the slightest smidge of satisfaction at having driven Elizabeth away. Maybe she'd seen a flash of the evil sorcerer in him.

When the meeting was finally over, all the students left for their afternoon classes, and Mr. Collins assured him that he had a place on the *Oracle* team should he choose to do so. Tobey politely declined, explaining about his situation at home. (Although if his mother kept taking business trips, he could probably do whatever he wanted.)

"Well, if anything changes, the door is always open," Mr. Collins said, his blue eyes crinkling up at the corners. Then the phone rang in his office. "Oh, excuse me a moment." He left, and Tobey gathered his papers.

As he stuffed them back in the folder, he found a scrap of paper underneath one page.

It was a note! From Quentin. Sighing with relief, he read it.

I'm sick today. Stuck in my house. Let's try to catch up tomorrow.

If Jessica asks, I'm not too sick to take her to the dance.

Tobey frowned. There was something odd about Quentin's handwriting. But he had no choice but to believe it. After all, who could forge a magical message?

In gym class, Coach Schultz chose Tobey to lead their brief warm-up exercises and then let him delegate which students were on each team. He was actually relieved, since without the ring he wouldn't be able to do as many pull-ups as he'd done before.

Tobey's Story

Charlie was conspicuously absent, and all the other boys seemed in awe of Tobey. They patted him on the back in the locker room as if he were one of the guys. Todd Wilson gave him a friendly smile.

When school let out for the day, Tobey dumped his books in his locker. He'd been carrying around the *Witchcraft* book, but with Quentin absent, there was no need. It would be safer in his locker, he decided. Once that was done, he headed out the front doors of the school. He saw Jessica leaving with Lila, but then she spotted him and ran over. "Have you heard anything from Quentin?" she asked, glancing back at her friend, who was standing there with her hands on her hips.

Tobey's lip curled. Of course she treated him like an equal now that she wanted something. A vision of him as the evil sorcerer sacrificing her on his altar flew through his mind—only now, Quentin was his magical accomplice. In his imagination, the witch boy and the sorcerer made fast work of poor, helpless Jessica.

Jessica was looking at him expectantly, so he came back to reality. He relayed Quentin's message, and she scampered off, looking relieved.

I should have told her he didn't want to speak to her ever again, he thought savagely. Even if it was a lie, the look on her face would have been priceless. But he had to trust that Quentin had his own plans for Jessica.

Outside the school building, he passed by the tree they'd met at earlier in the week. To his surprise, Tom McLay was standing there. Tom looked up when Tobey approached. "Hey," he grunted. "Uh, have you seen Quentin anywhere?"

"No," Tobey said. "He must be absent today." He wondered why Tom was so interested in the new boy.

"Oh, OK." Tom trudged away.

That was weird.

Since his mother was out of town, Tobey decided to pay a visit to Mr. August at the Book Cellar. Quentin's note had given him an odd feeling—instead of allaying his fears, it was stoking them. He couldn't shake the feeling that there was something wrong with Quentin.

He drove downtown, with Quentin's note on the dashboard. Maybe Mr. August could do some magic on it to determine Quentin's whereabouts.

He pulled up to the boutique, parked, and grabbed the note from his dashboard, hurrying down the set of concrete stairs.

The door to the Book Cellar was locked, and the inside was dark—darker than usual. He knocked on the door. "Mr. August?" he yelled.

No answer. He peered inside. There was no movement inside the store.

Where is he?

He wondered if anyone in the boutique upstairs could help him, and he ran back up the stairs. The contrast between gloomy basement bookstore interior and the surface sunshine was stark, and spots floated in front of his eyes briefly.

But Seraphina's door was also locked. He frowned as he glanced at the store hours on the sign in the window. It was *supposed* to be open. He knocked, but no one answered.

Defeated, he plodded back to his car.

When he dug the note out of his pocket and placed it on the passenger seat, it crumbled into dust. Tobey yelped in surprise.

Now I know something's wrong.

* * *

Quentin was dreaming, which was odd for having been knocked out. He was no longer in the kitchen, but in the parlor, the same parlor in which he'd tried to summon Tobey as the Hellcniht demon. The furniture had been moved aside, and the rug rolled back to make room for a circle marked on the wooden floor.

He could see his own prostate form lying in the center of the circle. This magic circle was vastly different from the pentacle he'd used to summon the Hellcniht, and different from the one Tobey had used to summon the Nyx. The star inside the circle had seven points instead of five, and the symbols in between the points were ones he didn't recognize.

Tobey's Story

August was standing on one side of the circle, wearing an amulet of some kind, and Maeve was directly across from him.

"Now, foul creature, take thy true form," August thundered, baring his teeth. The stone in his amulet glowed red.

Quentin's body in the pentacle began to glow bright green, and his dream self felt a wrenching in his stomach. He doubled over in agony. The light in the circle shone brighter, blinding him.

He awoke in the center of the circle. His head ached, and his body felt leaden.

At the same time, it felt... different. It wasn't Quentin's buff male teenage body anymore—it was the Nyx's curvaceous, ageless female demon body, hovering two feet off the floor. (Her feet were cloven hooves now, which was kind of interesting.)

The Nyx bared her jagged teeth and flexed her clawed fingers. She blinked her yellow eyes, and two adult figures came into view.

"Oh, this is just embarrassing," she groaned in her demon voice. Tobey's parents had never seen her in demon form. It was as if they had walked in Piper and Tobey... *consorting* on one of the witch's holy days.

"Back, foul demon," August boomed. "Ye are bound to this circle, and ye cannot escape."

"No shit," the Nyx said in her deep, guttural voice. "I'm not really a demon, you know. I'm a witch." She glanced around frantically, looking for something that could get her down. To her left, she could see a tall plant stand that hadn't been moved—on top of it was a small pot.

There was that *mentha piperita* again. What was it doing in the parlor? The light in the kitchen was better for growing plants...

"You lie," Maeve pronounced, stepping over to join her husband. They both peered up at the demon hovering in front of them. "Just like when you had us believe you were an ordinary mortal teenage boy!"

"A teenage boy who tried to seduce our son," August added.

"I wasn't trying to *seduce* him," the Nyx growled in annoyance, with a toss of her ram-horned head. "I was just trying to get him out of Saccharin Valley. Really, this has gone *way* too far..."

"Aye, I agree with you there," August said gravely. "I dabbled in sorcery, summoned demons like *you*, and paid the price. I left my family to protect my son... I didn't want him to go down the same path..."

"Ohhh," said the Nyx, her slit-pupil eyes lighting up with sudden understanding. "I thought y'all were just homophobes."

They glared at her.

"It's fine if you don't want your son to become a sorcerer... *in Saccharin Valley*. Back home, of course, he's already a powerful warlock, and you two are supportive of his endeavors... well, mostly."

"Silence your deceptive tongue, demon," Maeve commanded.

"I believe I am beholden to the spellcaster, only," smirked the Nyx. "So that means I obey August, not *you*, sweetie."

"In that you are correct," said August. "So it is *I* who will banish you from this plane, never to return."

The Nyx's yellow eyes widened in a demonic version of fear. "OK, hold on a damn minute! I just want to know one thing: how did Tobey end up here in the first place? I didn't send him, and Aetemus had nothing to do with it..."

"None of your tricks, vile serpent," Maeve spat. "Do it, August."

"I thought your name was *Mr.* August," the Nyx muttered. Hanging in the air, she feebly kicked her cloven hooves. "Aren't you the proprietor of the store that sold Tobey the very book that could summon me? That's really poor parenting, if you ask me."

"I made a mistake, and now I am rectifying it," August said, glowering. "Now, be gone!"

Glowing green light shot up from the circle, surrounding the Nyx. Now Tobey's parents were shadowy blurs.

"Oh, for real? After all I went through to get here?" she cried.

Tobey's Story

But the bright green light engulfed her, and she felt her demon body being pulled elsewhere.

In the last instant, she snatched a few leaves from the plant pot. If she was going to be banished to the underworld, she wanted to have fresh breath.

The pull strengthened, and she gasped.

Then everything went black.

*   *   *

Tobey awoke with a start, not knowing where he was for a moment. Then the events of the day came rushing back.

Quentin was still missing, the Book Cellar was closed, and he'd lost the ring the Nyx had given him.

It was Friday morning, the day of the Lucky 13 Dance. Quentin was taking Jessica—but he was setting her up for *something*.

And he couldn't summon the Nyx again until the next new moon.

He reached under his mattress for the *Witchcraft* book. It wasn't there. His blood ran cold. Where had he put it?

Then he remembered stuffing a bunch of books in his locker.

The book was at school.

He rolled over and groaned. He would have to go to school today. He didn't want to face anyone but Quentin. And he didn't want to go to class; he only wanted to consult the book—or Quentin, if he was there—on what to do next.

He'd made an utter mess of things.

Sighing, he got up and trudged into the bathroom. His reflection looked haggard, bleary-eyed. He felt like he'd been through the ringer—but how, why, he wasn't sure.

Chapter 11

Piper sat straight up in bed. "I am alive!" she crowed. Not only that, but her mouth tasted delightfully minty. "HA! Suck it, Saccharin Valley!"

That bit of *mentha piperita* had saved her from being banished into oblivion! It was the reminder of who she was, underneath the hunky teen boy, the demon, and Tobey's dream witch. She was a powerful enchantress, and though Saccharin Valley had bested her many times before, she'd always managed to wreak havoc and have a little fun before making her egress unscathed.

She jumped up out of her bed. Her feet met with an unfamiliar rug.

She turned to look at the bed, and realized it wasn't her bed.

It was Quentin's bed. She was still in Saccharin Valley.

"Dammit."

But there was sunlight streaming through the window. That was a good sign, right? No more vines, so no more wards. She could leave if she wanted to.

Wait, wasn't the window supposed to be on the other side of the room? She glanced around. The door was on the wrong side too.

The lighted vanity table was gone.

She ran into the bathroom. No mirror there either. What was going on?

She was in a mirror image of Quentin's bedroom... with no mirrors to show her what she looked like, or what her surroundings were *supposed* to look like.

"Trippy," she said.

She ran down two flights of stairs to the parlor where Maeve and August had banished the Nyx. All the furniture was back in place, and the rug, although this room had also been reversed. The whole house was flipped, now a reflection of its former self.

There was no sign of August or Maeve. The plant stand was still there, but the potted peppermint plant was missing.

Then she looked at the opposite wall—well, opposite opposite, now that it had been mirror-imaged. There was a framed large mirror there. She sighed in relief.

Her reflection showed a good-looking ginger-haired teenage boy, dressed for school in a T-shirt and jeans. Quentin Pepper.

But when she looked down, she saw that she was still Piper Quintin, in a female body, wearing a black dress, striped stockings, and pointy-toed granny boots.

She placed her hands on her breasts, and her reflection placed his hands on his pectorals.

"Oh, this is not good," she said.

Just then the phone rang, and Piper jumped. It was ringing in the mirror, but not in real life. She watched as Quentin, on the other side of the Looking-Glass, answered it.

"Hello? Oh, Tobey, hi. Yes, I'm OK. I just wasn't feeling well..."

Piper gaped as her mirror-image, gender-swapped twin had a whole conversation with *her* consort, Tobey North. Who didn't belong here in Saccharin Valley.

Quentin told Tobey that he was going to humiliate Jessica at the dance.

Tobey's Story

Hey, I want to do that! Piper thought angrily. *No, wait, I just want Tobey to remember who he is, and we can hightail it out of this sunny, saccharin hellscape.*

Quentin was listening to Tobey. Piper had the bright idea to pick up the phone on her side... now she could hear Tobey's side of the conversation, too.

"I lost the ring," Tobey said, his voice full of anguish. "And my book is in my locker. Not that I can really use it for anything—I can't summon the Nyx again until the next new moon."

"But you've survived at school before you had either the book *or* the ring," Quentin pointed out.

"Yeah, but not without a lot of pain," Tobey said bitterly. "Charlie's been pretty quiet lately. He has to be plotting something."

"Look, I've got to go or I'll be late for school again," Quentin said. "But you can stay home if you want. That way your bullies can't get you."

"No, I'll be there," Tobey said. "If you're going, I mean. Safety in numbers, I suppose."

"Or you could just stay home," Piper said into the phone. Neither boy heard her. "There's no reason to go to school. You're a warlock, not a high school boy!"

But Quentin had hung up. Piper watched as he walked toward the front hall, out of view of the mirror. She ran to the foyer, where there was a small mirror hanging on the wall over a little decorative wooden table.

"Where are you going?" she cried at her alter ego. She knew he was going to school, but since they'd split, it didn't seem like Quentin wanted to help Tobey anymore. The Quentin part of her, now separated, was simply a good-looking high school student (who also dabbled in magic), keen on attending Saccharin Valley High and doing normal teenage things.

She watched him leave, fists clenched in frustration.

Then she went to the closet off the kitchen and pulled out a broom.

"I may be in Saccharin Valley—a weird Looking-Glass version of Saccharin Valley—but I'm still a witch."

*   *   *

"Quentin! You made it!" Jessica shrieked as a bright red Jaguar pulled up beside the twins' Jeep.

"I'll see you in English," Elizabeth said, her blue-green eyes sparkling as she exited the Jeep. She watched as Jessica, ignoring her, ran over to Quentin and threw herself into his arms. Then, laughing, Elizabeth locked the car and headed toward the school entrance, where Enid and Todd were waiting.

"You're not contagious, are you?" Jessica said, pulling away from Quentin, who had ducked his head down for a kiss.

He laughed. "No, I'm not contagious," he said.

"Good," Jessica replied, and they made out.

In the rearview mirror of the Jaguar, a witch sat perched on the tiny back seat, unnoticed by either of them. Once in the air, she'd noticed there was a sort of invisible tether connecting her with her male, Saccharin Valley counterpart, and her broom was pulled along like a kite on a string. She'd swooped down when he parked.

"Come on, let's go to homeroom," Quentin said. "I have a surprise for you."

"Ooh, a surprise? For me?" Jessica's chatter faded out as she and Quentin entered the school. From her place in the mirror realm, Piper followed, feeling a tug whenever Quentin walked too far away from her.

She glanced back at the parking lot, seeing Tobey's Toyota pull into a parking space on the other side of Quentin's car. He must've decided to come to school after all.

In another corner of the parking lot, Charlie, Aaron, and Bruce were plotting something.

Tobey skulked into homeroom just as the bell rang, after checking his locker to make sure the book was still in there. He transferred it to his backpack for safekeeping. No one paid him any attention, which was refreshing, although the change in the teachers' attitude from yesterday to today was so swift, it felt like whiplash.

He watched in homeroom as Quentin and Jessica leaned into each other, whispering. Quentin had pulled out a velvet jewelry box, and Jessica was exclaiming in delight.

It was a diamond tennis bracelet. Where had Quentin gotten such a thing? Was there a spell in his copy of the book to summon expensive jewelry?

Elizabeth saw this and her mouth hung open for a moment, before she turned back around. She caught Tobey's eye and gave him a look of sympathy.

He stared stonily back. *I don't need your pity,* he thought. He could feel his heart hardening into the wicked sorcerer that he was meant to be.

He glanced back over to Jessica and Quentin. He couldn't wait for tonight. Forget revenge on his bullies; he wanted to see Jessica suffer.

Piper watched in dismay from the girls' bathroom mirror as several students she didn't care about gossiped and put on makeup. It didn't seem like girls actually used the bathroom in these books, despite there being functioning toilets.

She waited for Jessica to appear, having stretched the invisible tether as far as it would go, but Jessica must've not needed to pee this morning, so she flitted into the boys' bathroom to watch for Quentin. This morning she'd been able to watch Tobey from his locker mirror. He had taken the book out of his locker and transferred it to his book bag. That was good, Piper decided. Maybe she could influence him to summon her as the Nyx again? But Tobey couldn't see or hear her, and in this mirror-reflection form, she didn't seem to have any of the abilities that Quentin had gotten from his *Witchcraft* book.

To her incredible luck, both Tobey and Quentin met in a seldom-used boys' bathroom on the third floor between periods.

"I have the book," Tobey said once he'd checked the stalls and locked the door.

"I won't need it," Quentin said confidently, preening in the mirror.

Why can't Tobey tell it's not me? Piper raged silently. He didn't seem to think anything about Quentin was out of the ordinary.

"So, what are you going to do?"

Quentin smiled at his reflection while putting gel in his hair. "I don't need magic to humiliate Jessica," he said. "I've got it all planned out. I'm going to dazzle her, show her a good time, be the perfect boyfriend... and then, at the end of the dance, dump her in front of everybody."

Tobey pursed his lips, looking pensive. Piper could tell he was wondering why Quentin's plan was so *ordinary*—something a mere mortal could do. If he was a witch, why wouldn't he cast a really heinous spell on Jessica instead?

Of course, having seen the book, Piper knew there weren't any revenge spells in there.

"Plus, I made a date with Tom McLay on the same night," Quentin went on. "Jessica will be horrified to learn she's being dumped for a good-looking *boy!*"

"That doesn't seem very fair to Tom," Tobey said quietly.

"Well, he's gay in a small California town... beggars can't be choosers." Quentin was now inspecting his perfect teeth in the mirror.

You absolute clod, Piper thought, seething. *She* wanted to be the one to see Jessica's face when Quentin dumped her. *She* wanted to be the one to humiliate Jessica! Then she shook her head, putting her face in her hands. This was ridiculous. She didn't need to torment Jessica... she just needed to get Tobey out of here. Usually Piper reveled in chaos, but this unexpected detour was making her tired.

The boys left the bathroom, and Piper, frustrated, picked up the trash can on her side and slammed it into the mirror. To her surprise, it cracked. She could feel fresh air coming from the normal Saccharin Valley side.

She put her hand up to the crack. Hmmm.

* * *

Tobey's Story

Tobey moved through his school day like a ghost, swimming through the crowds of students in the halls, acknowledging no one. Everywhere he went, it seemed like Charlie and his friends were lurking—but they always seemed to be leaving just as he noticed them. It made him uneasy that they weren't openly taunting him.

At lunch, Quentin was sitting with Jessica and her friends again. He thought about joining them, but something made him change his mind, so he went to his usual table in the far corner of the cafeteria and sat with his lunch box unopened, deep in thought.

Quentin was busy with his revenge plan on Jessica, and so he couldn't help Tobey with any other spells. Tobey couldn't summon the Nyx again for another three weeks, and the ring was still lost, so he couldn't change its purpose again. What was he supposed to do? It all felt so anticlimactic. He'd thought summoning a demon would give him enough power that he could end his bullies in a spectacular fashion, and take control of his life, once and for all.

At the end of the lunch period, Quentin got up from Jessica's table and fell into step with Tobey. He didn't seem to be in any hurry, which was unusual considering how he'd acted the last few days.

"So," Quentin said, "Are you coming to the dance? I'd love for you to witness my evil plan coming to fruition." His hazel eyes glinted with merriment.

"I don't have a date," Tobey sighed.

"It doesn't matter," Quentin said. "Come stag. You have such a great style, I'd love to see what you would wear to such a cheesy event."

Tobey smiled a little, remembering his earlier fantasy. "What are *you* going to wear?"

"Oh, Jessica has it all picked out," Quentin said, rolling his eyes. "But I'll try to add some of my own flair to the ensemble."

"I *would* go," Tobey said, his brow furrowing. "But I feel like Charlie is plotting something. Every time I see him, he's with Bruce and Aaron, and they're whispering."

"Can't you summon your demon again?" Quentin asked.

"Not until the new moon," Tobey said.

"There's got to be something in your book that can help you."

Tobey shook his head. "It's all folklore. Everything magic I could do, came from the demon." He frowned, thinking of the way he'd scared Bruce off, and made Elizabeth leave the *Oracle* office.

They'd reached Tobey's locker, and Tobey dumped his books in, including the *Witchcraft* book.

"You keep your book at school?" Quentin said, raising his eyebrows.

"Don't you have somewhere to be?" Tobey countered, looking around nervously. Were the "spies" Quentin had told him about here with them, among the throng of students?

"No, not really," Quentin said. "I figured out a trick to keep the spies off my tail. It was something in my copy of the book."

"Do you have it with you?" Tobey asked. Maybe there was something in Quentin's copy that could help him finish off the bullies once and for all.

Quentin shook his head. "It's at home."

"Oh," Tobey said. The bell was about to ring—he had to get to gym class. "I have to go, but can you do something for me?"

Quentin looked at him. "Sure."

"Look me in the eyes," Tobey instructed. "Tell me if you see anything... *unusual*."

Quentin was surprised, but only for an instant. "Sure," he said. He faced Tobey, there in the hall with all the students around them, hurrying to class or to their lockers.

Tobey took a deep breath, centering himself. The noise of the students faded to the background as he summoned all of his sorcerer energy, willing it into his eyes. They began to prickle, as they had before.

Quentin backed up a little. "Is something supposed to happen?" he asked, bewildered.

Tobey exhaled. His friend couldn't see the wicked sorcerer behind his eyes. His shoulders slumped.

"No, I guess not," he said.

The bell rang, and he turned abruptly, hurrying to gym class.

Quentin stared after him, shrugged, then walked in the opposite direction.

*   *   *

In Tom McLay's Chemistry class, Mr. Russo had them brighten up old pennies in a mixture of salt and vinegar for the dance. Quentin joined Tom at his lab table. While they were doing the experiment, they chatted as if they were friends—*just* friends—but whenever Quentin's hand brushed against his, he felt a tingle.

When class was over, they all gathered up their pennies, which they'd dried on paper towels, and put them in a large pickle jar Mr. Russo had on his desk.

"The dance committee thanks you for your service," he told them.

Quentin ran out the door just as the bell rang, and Tom was left to clean up their lab station.

Under a damp paper towel, he spied a note.

See you at the dance.

He smiled, snatched up the note, and tucked it into his pocket.

Piper spent the rest of the school day on edge. It was dark and empty in the school on this side of the mirror. The only light came from the mirrors—in the bathrooms and in people's lockers. Quentin hadn't used the bathroom since that morning. Piper could follow him around in this dull, gray, mirror world, but she was like a shadow to him. She couldn't touch him or influence him, and she was completely shut off from Tobey.

She hovered near Quentin's car at the end of the day. The fact that she'd been able to break the bathroom mirror had given her an idea... but she'd need Quentin to be in front of a mirror for it to work.

Quentin and Jessica were walking hand-in-hand to the Jaguar.

"I'm *so* excited for tonight," Jessica bubbled.

Yawn, Piper thought.

"I'll pick you up at seven," Quentin told her.

She waved and walked over to where Elizabeth was sitting in the Jeep.

Once she was gone, Quentin angled the rearview mirror towards his face, checking his hair.

I was never this vain when I was you, Piper thought, annoyed.

She saw his hazel eyes gleam. Since they'd been separated, Quentin's eyes no longer gleamed green on occasion. Piper was hoping Tobey would notice, but if he did, he must not have thought anything of it.

Quentin started the car. The stereo was blasting "Mirror in the Bathroom" by The English Beat.

"How apropos," Piper said. Of course, Quentin didn't hear her.

He revved the engine and pulled out of the parking lot.

The whole ride home, Piper tried to break the rearview mirror. But it was tricky, the way it was angled. She discovered she couldn't occupy the same space as Quentin at the same time, so she was sitting in the passenger seat, rooting through the glove box on her side of the mirror.

Quentin didn't keep anything in there that was heavy enough to crack the mirror. He weaved in and out of traffic on the freeway, and it made Piper nauseous. When they were behind a truck, a pebble kicked up from the vehicle's mud flaps flew up and struck the windshield, making a tiny crack.

If only I could affect its trajectory, Piper thought. Back in the Witch World, psychokinesis was easy-peasy, one of the first spells a fledgling witch was taught. But here in Saccharin Valley, trapped in a reflection, she might as well be mortal.

Quentin took an off-ramp, and Piper sat back in her seat, panting. She wasn't able to move any pebbles, and the effort had left her winded. The motion of the car,

Tobey's Story

and the breeze from the top being down, made her sleepy.

When Quentin pulled into the driveway, he turned off the car, checking his reflection in the side mirror.

The side mirror! Piper sat straight up. She had one shot. She pulled the lever to recline the seat, drew up one leg, and kicked the mirror on her side with her witch boot's heel.

To her surprise, it cracked. The noise jolted her out of her stupor. She kicked again, making more cracks.

Quentin exited on his side, but when he heard the mirror crack, he dashed over to the passenger side.

"What the—?"

Piper was frantically pulling at the shattered pieces of glass, wrenching them out of the side mirror casing. Finally, it was just a hole. A hole she could reach through.

When Quentin bent down to examine the damage, she lunged.

Quentin yelped in surprise, trying to remove himself from her grip, but she held fast. She could feel his aura, and she grabbed onto that, breathing it in, absorbing it.

Quentin struggled, trying to throw her off, but she was like a dog with a bone. She would not fail this time. She *had* to get Tobey and take him home.

As her aura melded with Quentin's, she could hear someone screaming. Was it her, or her mirror twin? Quentin bucked like a wild bronco, but Piper was an expert rider. With one final heave, Quentin lost his balance and fell to the ground.

Then they both blacked out.

*   *   *

When Tobey got home from school, the house was empty and silent. His mother would be back later tonight. He sank into a chair, happy to be free of bullies, magic gone wrong, and his mother's questions. And free from watching his new friend dote on Jessica.

He started to get sleepy. He usually wasn't one for naps, but the chair was comfy, and he didn't have to do anything or be anywhere.

He sighed and got comfortable. Within minutes, he was asleep.

The dream witch was back. Tobey was surprised to see her. So much had happened, he felt shy.

"Piper," he said.

"Hi, Tobey," she said, with a warm smile. Her eyes glittered like emeralds—the same shade of green, he realized, that Quentin's had looked under certain light. At least, he'd *thought* they had—having seen them today, they'd been dull hazel the whole time.

Maybe he'd imagined the whole thing.

"We really don't have much time," she said.

He looked around. They were in a lavish bedroom in the turret of an old Victorian house. He could see the sky outside the large window—it was a swirling multicolored galaxy, unlike anything he'd seen before.

"Why not?" he asked. "No one's coming for us... no one knows we're here..."

"I can't stay here long, and neither can you," she said. Outside the window, the stars in the galaxy whizzed by. It made him dizzy. "But if you go to the dance tonight, I can fix things."

"The dance? But I don't have a date, or something cool to wear..."

"Just go," she said. "I'll take care of everything."

"But I don't have the ring..."

A strong breeze blew the curtain in front of the chair she was sitting in, obscuring her from view. When they settled down, she was gone.

Just go, please, a voice echoed in his mind.

Chapter 12

"How'd you get his locker open?" Aaron Dulles wanted to know. He, Charlie, and Bruce were standing in front of Tobey's locker, the door of which was gaping, and the combination lock lying open on the floor.

It was late Friday afternoon, and most of the lights were out in the hall. All the other students had gone home to get ready for the dance. But these three boys had a bone to pick with Tobey North.

Charlie grunted. "I may have a black eye, but my fingers still work," he said. "I picked the lock, of course." He started pulling stuff out of the locker—schoolbooks, papers, pens, a jacket that looked like it was from the 60s—and flinging them to the floor. The heavier items landed with thuds that echoed through the hall.

"Keep it down, would you?" Bruce muttered. "There might be some teachers still here."

"Not any in this wing," Aaron told him. "I checked."

Charlie was sweeping his hand over the top shelf of the locker, and pulled out an antique silver comb. "Gay," Charlie muttered, tossing the comb aside. "There must be *something* incriminating in here..."

Aaron knelt down to go through the pile of things Charlie had tossed aside. "Hey, guys," he said, picking up a small leather-bound book. "Look at this!"

They all stared at the creepy book.

"I knew he was a freak, but I didn't know he was into *black magic!*" Charlie exclaimed.

"You can't be serious," Bruce said. "This is all nonsense. Superstition and folklore."

"I don't know, it looks pretty real to me," Aaron said, paging through the book. There were lines of fancy script and sinister-looking diagrams throughout the book.

"Is *that* how he was so strong a couple of days ago?" Charlie muttered to himself. He reached up with his fingertips to gingerly touch his black eye, which was starting to turn green. Tobey was usually a wimp, so his sudden agility *had* to be the result of a spell.

"I thought you said you got into a fight with someone *outside* of school," Bruce said, with a grin of realization on his face.

Before Charlie could answer, the book caught fire in his hands. Charlie screamed and chucked the burning book back into the locker, where the remaining papers immediately ignited. "Oh, crap!" he said.

"Fire!" Aaron yelled. "We're going to get in so much trouble!" He started picking Tobey's things from the floor and tossing them into the locker... causing the blaze to grow bigger.

"You idiot!" Bruce cried. He ran to get the fire extinguisher from the glass case set in the wall, came hurrying back, pulled the pin, squeezed the handle, and white foam spewed into Tobey's locker, smothering the flames.

"Phew," Aaron said. He stood up shakily, brushing flecks of foam off his jeans.

"What a mess," Bruce said, standing back and shaking his head. "Well, you guys can get this cleaned up —I have to get ready for the dance. I have a hot date."

Aaron and Charlie squawked with protest, but Bruce had already disappeared down the dark hall.

Tobey's Story

"What a jerk," Charlie muttered. He slammed the locker door shut on the foamy mess, and replaced the lock, clicking it closed.

Aaron gathered the last few pieces of paper from the floor and threw them in a trash bin outside the boys' bathroom.

He heard whistling from inside, and froze. A toilet flushed.

"It's the janitor!" he hissed to Charlie. "Let's get out of here!"

They ran.

When Mr. Jensen exited the restroom, he saw bits of foam dripping from one student's locker and frowned. "What on earth?" He grabbed his mop.

There was a piece of paper on the floor a little ways down, and he picked it up to throw away.

It was a drawing—a really good drawing of a fantasy character, an evil sorcerer. But the edges were singed.

He shrugged and tossed it in his rolling trash can.

*   *   *

Quentin had a massive headache, but at least he remembered that he was Piper. Looking up at the exterior of the house, he was relieved to see that there were no thorny vines covering the windows.

No wards prevented his entry. No fake Tobey's parents were lurking in the kitchen.

The clock over the stove said five p.m.—how long had he been out?

He checked each floor for intruders, but found nobody. It was quiet, but the quiet was peaceful, not dangerous.

Just to be sure Tobey's parents were gone, he grabbed a phone book from inside a cabinet and flipped through it until he found the number for the Book Cellar. The phone beeped and said the number was no longer in service.

Good, he thought. He still had his book. He just didn't want August (or *Mr.* August) coming after him.

And what about Maeve? He flipped more pages, found the number for Rowan. At lunch, when he'd joined Jessica and her friends, Lila couldn't stop talking about the store she'd found, and Quentin remembered her description of the owner. Plus, what were the chances there were *two* people named Maeve in Saccharin Valley?

The phone rang two times, then a recorded message said Seraphina's was closed.

Fine, he thought, standing in the middle of the kitchen, with his feet planted, trying to ground himself. This body felt different, but he was able to take a deep breath, pausing when his lungs were full, then exhaling completely.

What now? It was all going down at the dance. He'd have to play along until he could find Tobey.

If he'd decided to come.

Quentin was ravenous from his stint in the Looking-Glass, so he fixed himself a snack. Food was the best way to replenish his energy—now that it wasn't bespelled Fey food. He couldn't risk taking a nap, given what had happened last time he'd gone to sleep.

Once he was satiated, he went upstairs to get ready for the dance.

*   *   *

Tom McLay tied a bow tie using the mirror in the bathroom. He was so excited to meet Quentin at the dance. *I can't believe he said yes!* Quentin had confided to him that he *wasn't* interested in Tobey after all—Tobey was straight, and Quentin just wanted to borrow some history notes off him. Tom didn't have any other classes with Quentin besides Chemistry, so he hadn't seen much of him in the last few days.

He couldn't wait to be alone with him.

Tom grabbed his keys and said goodbye to his parents, who thought he was meeting his date (a girl) at the dance.

"You look sharp," his mother said, smiling.

His dad peered over the top of his newspaper. "A chip off the ol' block," he agreed, appreciating the perfectly tied bowtie. "I taught you well." He didn't comment on the color—the bowtie was lavender.

Tom grabbed his keys and headed to his car.

Jessica, meanwhile, was thrilled to be going to the dance with Quentin Pepper. She'd gotten to know him in the past few days, and he'd found out that he liked playing tennis, dancing at the Beach Disco, and driving at night with the top down.

Most importantly, he always heaped praise on her, telling her how beautiful she was, and how fabulous.

He was perfect for her.

She was filled with excitement while she got ready for the dance. She spent an extra twenty minutes in the mirror, artfully applying her makeup. Then she slid into her new dress, loving the feel of the material against her skin. She styled her hair, and fastened the diamond tennis bracelet on her wrist. It sparkled in the bathroom lights.

"Wow," Elizabeth said when she saw her sister come into the living room. She had finished getting ready thirty minutes ago and was sitting on the couch waiting for Todd. "That dress looks incredible on you."

"I know, right?" Jessica said with a toss of her head. "Quentin's going to *die* when he sees me!"

"Hopefully, he won't be too deceased to dance with you," Elizabeth teased.

After Elizabeth had left for the dance with Todd, a red Jaguar convertible XJS drove up to the curb at the Wastefeld's house.

Quentin came inside to meet Jessica's parents. He was polite and utterly charming. He told Jessica she looked stunning in her new dress. He even knew the correct terminology—he'd said *flounce* instead of *ruffle*. He was dressed in a navy suit with a brocade vest that was the same hue as Jessica's dress, a matching purple shirt, and a copper-colored tie.

(Jessica had worried a bit that he was actually gay, but gay people were only mentioned a few times in over one hundred books, so she knew that statistically speaking, he *had* to be only interested in girls. And he was *clearly* interested in one girl in particular—her.)

Quentin handed her a clear box. Inside was a corsage with an orchid that matched the color of the dress exactly.

"Oh, this is perfect!" Jessica squealed. She let the hunky boy pin it on her—he got it positioned correctly on the first try and didn't stick her with the pin.

"Have fun!" said Mr. and Mrs. Wastefeld as Jessica and her date made their way down the driveway to Quentin's car.

*   *   *

The gym looked amazing. It had been completely transformed into a magical realm of luck and good fortune. The dance committee had put up silver and gold streamers, white, silver, and gold balloons, and hung oversized twinkling stars from the ceiling. There were rainbows painted across the walls. In the corner was a wishing well that participants could throw lucky pennies into, and then have their photos taken under an arch next to a pot of gold.

The 7-ingredient punch was streaming out of a tiered crystal fountain. Lucky desserts were piled around it—donuts (the ring shape symbolized the cyclical nature and fullness of life), a cake with tiny surprises baked inside, and a platter of fortune cookies.

Jessica always reveled in first entering the Saccharin Valley High School gym for a dance. Everyone always turned to look at her, in awe of her beauty, her fabulous dress, and her hunky date.

Tonight was no exception. She held onto Quentin's arm possessively as she smiled and waved at all her friends.

"Oh, here comes Lila and her date," he said.

Jessica sucked in her breath as Lila entered the gym, with an incredibly handsome older boy. He looked like a model for the cover of a romance novel. Broad-shouldered, well-muscled, with shoulder-length dark-blonde hair and big blue eyes. There was something funny about those eyes—the irises were a little too big. He was wearing a designer suit and smiling politely.

Lila approached, clutching her date's arm, a smug look on her face. "Jessica, this is Rowan Berry, the boy I told you about," she purred.

"Nice to meet you," Jessica said dutifully. "This is *my* new boyfriend, Quentin Pepper."

Quentin looked from Jessica to Lila, and his hazel eyes gleamed. They somehow looked green in the light from the hanging stars. He took Lila's hand briefly, and he and Rowan exchanged curt nods.

Satisfied that she'd one-upped Jessica with the attractiveness of her date, Lila cried, "Let's dance!"

She and Rowan moved to the center of the dance floor, where all eyes would be on them.

Jessica turned to Quentin with a little laugh. "Don't pay any attention to her," she told him. "She's just jealous of us."

Quentin's curiously green eyes shone. "Your friend seems a little... competitive," he remarked. "How do you stand it? I thought the point of a dance was to have a good time."

"I know, right?" Jessica said airily, as if she wasn't *exactly* the same as Lila when it came to dating and dances. "It's sickening. But anyway, come on, let's show them how it's done."

She dragged him onto the dance floor, right next to Lila and Rowan, and started dancing for her life. To her utmost satisfaction, Quentin immediately joined in.

He was a really good dancer, she saw. He knew all the latest steps and could keep up with her without taking all the attention off her.

She was in heaven.

*   *   *

Tobey arrived at the school dressed in an outfit straight from the 70s—a burnt-orange suit and a paisley shirt with a dagger collar, and two-toned platform loafers. Dressing for the dance was like putting on his battle armor. He'd awoken from his nap with the strong desire to see Quentin's plan for Jessica play out. And he wanted to look through the book one more time, to see if there was anything crucial that he'd missed.

He ran to his locker and spun the combination lock, missing the correct number the first two times because his hands were shaking.

When he finally got his locker open, the smell that hit his nostrils wasn't frog juice—it smelled like something burnt.

The inside of his locker had been trashed; several things were missing. There were burn marks streaking the metal interior, and an odd gummy residue coated the things that remained.

In the bottom of his locker was a charred lump—the *Witchcraft* book. "No," he whispered, picking it up. The pages were blackened beyond recognition and crumbling into ash. Without the ring, he didn't have power, but without the book, he couldn't *get* more power.

He threw the book back inside, closed the locker door, and kicked it. What was he going to do? Sure, he'd had some fun already, but now that he had a taste of power, he didn't want to let it go. There were still people he wanted to make pay.

For now, it would suffice to watch Jessica suffer at the hands of his new friend—but he'd have to go to the dance and pretend like he was having fun until the very end.

And he'd have to avoid Charlie, Bruce, and Aaron. He was still convinced they weren't done with him.

Steeling his resolve, he turned and headed back down the hall towards the gym.

Olivia smiled shyly at Tobey as he walked past her. "Oh, Tobey, I *love* your outfit!" She was dressed in a paisley-print hippie maxi dress—it was almost as if they matched.

He stopped, feeling a pang in his heart. Maybe they would've been a couple if he'd been normal and not a freak-turned-sorcerer. "Listen, Olivia, I just wanted to say I'm sorry I couldn't take you to the dance. You're a

Tobey's Story

great girl, but I've got a lot of personal stuff going on right now..."

"How did you know I wanted to ask you?" Olivia said incredulously.

Tobey paused, realizing she'd never actually asked him to the dance. He'd just known. He shrugged. "Just a hunch."

"Anyway, it's all right. Aaron told me what's going on."

"He... did?" Tobey said. Aaron was one of his bullies, so that didn't seem right.

"And I just want to say, I hope you find someone special," she went on.

He looked at her, confused.

"You have a great style, Tobey, and I'm happy for you. There aren't many students at this school who are not afraid to be their *true* selves..."

He was bewildered. Who exactly did she think he was?

Did she somehow know he was a dabbler in witchcraft and summoner of demons?

"Have you talked to Tom McLay? *He's* gay, so I bet he knows what you're going through..."

Tobey reddened slightly. Oh. She thought he was *gay*. He remembered Quentin's hand on his leg in the library. He wasn't as bothered by this as the other Saccharin Valley High boys would've been.

At the same time, he didn't have time to stay and chat.

"Sorry, I have to go," he said, rushing off.

*   *   *

Quentin had just finished a dance with Jessica when he spotted Tom entering the gym through the far side doors.

"I'll be right back," he said to Jessica.

"Would you bring me a cup of punch?" Jessica asked.

"Sure."

He walked over to Tom, who smiled hesitantly when he saw him. Quentin pulled him into one of the equipment rooms.

"You made it," he said, grinning.

"How's Jessica?" Tom asked pointedly.

"She's... *Jessica*," Quentin said, with a helpless shrug, and they both laughed. "Honestly, she's a bit much."

"I don't doubt it." Tom looked at him hesitantly. "So, that's it? You dance all night with Jessica, and we pretend like we don't know each other?"

"I'm sorry," Quentin said, his shoulders drooping. "Jessica's waiting for me. You can come inside and dance, but it's better that you pretend you don't know me... like that."

Tom clenched his fists. The euphoria from having a secret date to the dance was fizzling out. "This sucks," he said finally. He kicked the wall of the equipment room.

"I know," Quentin said, a sad look in his eyes. "But I'll save a dance for you in the parking lot later. And we'll get together on the weekend and play tennis." With that, he leaned in for a kiss. Tom had never kissed a boy before—it felt amazing. Everything he didn't feel from kissing a girl, he felt now. Tingles all over. His heart thumping in his chest. Feeling giddy and lightheaded.

"Wow," Tom breathed when they broke apart. "That was amazing."

"Thanks," Quentin said, his hazel eyes crinkling up at the corners. "You weren't so bad yourself. I'll see you in an hour."

Tom couldn't help but smile. "I'll be waiting," he said.

Quentin gave Tom an awkward hug, then turned to leave. "That bowtie looks fabulous, by the way," he said over his shoulder.

* * *

Tobey had finally spotted Quentin in the crowd of dancing teenagers. But as he tried to make his way

Tobey's Story

over to where the ginger boy was dancing—with Jessica—his path was blocked by a group of boys.

Charlie Cashbox, Bruce Fatcat, and Aaron Dulles were all standing there, with menacing looks on their faces.

This was it. They were going to do something terrible. He was sure of it. He froze, unable to do anything to stop them.

"Get him," Charlie said.

Without the ring, of course, Tobey couldn't fight back. Not for lack of trying—he struggled in their grip, but they were too strong. They dragged him out of the main part of the gym and into a storage closet where sports equipment was kept, then stripped him down to his briefs and locked him in.

"Serves you right, freak," Charlie said.

The three boys' laughter echoed outside the door.

Tobey rattled the doorknob, but it was no use. He was trapped.

Chapter 13

Quentin had an unsettled feeling in his stomach... He hadn't seen Tobey yet, but he could feel that the blue-eyed boy was here at the school, and there was definitely something wrong. He ran to the bathroom—trying to stave off the dizziness from it being the other way around now that he was on the right side of the mirror—and shut himself in a stall to open his Third Eye.

One of the things he'd done before he left the house was make sure he could still use the spells in his copy of the book.

It was dimly lit where Tobey was... he seemed to be inside a closet where gym equipment was stored. What was he doing in there?

Also... he was wearing only his underwear. Where had his clothes gone?

Quentin watched him rattle the door, to no avail. Someone had locked him in. Had his bullies finally caught up with him? Was he really completely powerless without the ring?

This is not good, he thought.

First Tobey would need some clothes, Quentin decided. He attempted a translocation spell, something from the book, which he'd tucked into his suit jacket pocket.

Inside the tiny storage closet, something dropped from above, startling Tobey as it draped over his head. He pulled it off and looked at it in astonishment—it was his father's robe.

Quentin winced seeing how his spell had turned out. Ever since he'd come to Saccharin Valley, as a *boy*, his magic hadn't quite worked the way he wanted. And especially not since coming back from Looking-Glass Saccharin Valley. He saw Tobey decide that it was better than nothing, and put it on.

Something small rolled off the edge of a shelf and hit the floor with a *plink*. Tobey picked it up—it was a piece of chalk.

"Is that you, Mistress Nyx?" he whispered.

Quentin projected his voice into Tobey's head. There was that spell in the book for how to communicate with animals... and humans were *technically* animals.

Summon me, said the Nyx. *I can help you.*

Beads of sweat broke out on Quentin's forehead. Time was running out—he wasn't sure how much more magic he could use before he lost it all.

"But I can't," Tobey moaned. "It's not the new moon anymore... and anyway, my book was destroyed."

You don't need the book, whispered the voice. *You know my summoning by heart.*

As for the moon, it matters not—a mere technicality to deter neophytes. We are past that now, my boy. You and I have a strong connection.

Tobey looked like he was going to argue, but then realization dawned on his face. He *did* know it by heart. The pentacle, with its symbols, appeared in his mind, and the Latin words shimmered in the air before his eyes.

And if the Nyx told him he had the power to summon her, he believed her.

He knelt to the cement floor and began drawing the pentacle. Only, there wasn't enough space in here to step aside, so he ended up drawing it around himself.

It turned out much smaller than usual, but every symbol was correct. He spoke the words, and the symbols began to glow.

I hope this works.

Tobey's Story

*   *   *

The image of Tobey in Quentin's mind blinked out then, as if someone had turned out the lights. He opened his two regular eyes and realized what had interrupted his psychic vision—the door to the bathroom slamming open.

He could hear a boy using one of the urinals.

I'd better get back to Jessica, he thought.

Flushing the toilet for good measure, he opened the door to the stall.

Bruce Fatcat was at the sink washing his hands (for once). He caught sight of Quentin in the mirror and shot him a smug grin. "Very impressive, landing Jessica Wastefeld for a date," he said. "It's really funny how she has no idea what you *really* are."

Quentin said nothing, but his eyes glittered darkly. *You have no idea.*

"I'm sure she *loves* talking with you," Bruce went on in a taunting tone. "You two must have *so* much to talk about: fashion, *boys*..."

Quentin tried to leave, but Bruce swiftly stepped between him and the door.

"I bet you bought her a really nice corsage with the money I gave you," he went on. "But I wouldn't get too *cocky*"—here Bruce smiled, possibly considering that last word and what else it could refer to—"because, remember... I *own* you. One step out of line and I'll tell everyone who you are."

Quentin's eyes glowed green, and Bruce took a step back nervously.

Before Bruce could react, Quentin grabbed him by the collar—and kissed him on the lips. Then he threw the older boy against the wall and sashayed out.

Tobey raced down the hall, hoping he'd thrown his bullies off his scent. He'd done the ritual, exactly like before. But no Nyx had appeared (he'd even squished himself into the corner of the storage closet, to make room for her to come up through the center of the smaller-than-usual pentacle). However, *some* good had come of it—the force of the summoning magic had blown the door to his prison off its hinges. So at least he was free.

He pushed open the door to the gym, forgetting that he was still in his father's robe. He scanned the dance floor for Quentin, hoping the new boy could help him.

His eyes fell on the end of the stage—where his bullies were waiting.

"There's the freak," he could see Charlie say to Aaron, pointing. "How did he get out?"

Tobey brushed the chalk dust off his hands and put his bleeding finger in his mouth (he'd had to stab himself with the point of a pencil he'd found on a lower shelf, since there was nothing else sharp to use).

Now would be a good time to show up, he thought. Where was the Nyx?

The bullies saw him and came running.

*   *   *

"*There* you are," Jessica said when Quentin had rejoined her in the gym. She was holding a cup of lucky-seven punch. "Where were you? They played my favorite song while you were gone, and I had to dance with Ken."

"Sorry," Quentin muttered. "I was in the bathroom."

"No worries," Jessica said with a dazzling smile. "I got my own punch." She took his hand, but not before noticing how disheveled he looked.

"Are you OK? You're not getting sick again, are you?"

"No, I'm fine. It's just a little too hot in here." Quentin took his jacket off and draped it over the back of a folding metal chair, then loosened his tie.

"One more dance, just for me?" Jessica asked, batting her eyelashes coquettishly.

Quentin smiled wearily. "For you? Of course."

After the song was over, she said, "I'm going to say hi to Cara, and then we should get our picture taken by the wishing well."

Tobey's Story

"Sure," Quentin said, but his head was swiveled in the opposite direction, looking over at the end of the stage.

Tobey struggled in his captor's arms. Charlie was holding one arm, and Aaron the other. Any minute now Bruce would come and punch him in the stomach... unless being rich meant he'd outsourced the job.

"Look at this clown," Charlie said. "Why is he dressed for a Renaissance Faire?"

The other boys snorted with laughter. "He must've raided the drama club costume closet."

No other students noticed Tobey's plight, as they were all on the dance floor having a good time. Even the chaperones were facing in the other direction, oblivious to the bullying.

A door opened from across the gym, and a spotlight shone on the person in the doorway.

It was Quentin Pepper.

Jessica looked up from her place by the food table, where she'd been chatting with Cara. He must've gone outside to get some air, but why did he have a spotlight on him?

She watched the spotlight following Quentin as he strolled up to Tobey.

"Leave him to me, boys," Quentin said, a wicked gleam in his eyes. He cracked his knuckles.

To Tobey's surprise, they let go. Tobey saw that Quentin's eyes were glowing green. Had the Nyx finally shown up, in disguise? And if so, why was she disguised as the new boy? Tobey had been looking for him, and now here he was... looking like he wanted to pummel Tobey.

Tobey gave Quentin a pleading look. *Not you too,* he thought. *Not after we shared occult knowledge!*

Quentin clenched his fists, and Tobey began to get nervous. If it *was* the Nyx, what was she doing? He recalled Mr. August's words: *Demons are sneaky. You can't be too careful.*

Had the Nyx finally turned against him? But then why had she helped him get out of the closet?

Charlie, Aaron, and Bruce, as if dazed, retreated into the shadows of the corner of the gym, leaving their victim with Quentin.

Now the spotlight shone on Quentin and Tobey —one in a purple brocade vest and a copper tie, and one dressed in some sort of medieval sorcerer's robe. Before Tobey could react, Quentin Pepper lunged—and gathered Tobey in his arms, kissing him passionately on the lips.

Everyone stopped dancing and stared at them. Even the music cut out with the sound of a record scratch.

"Two boys kissing!" they whispered in shock. They had never seen such a thing. It was too weird.

"Gross," murmured Caroline Pierced.

Although one student was frowning for a different reason. It was unbelievable, Tom McLay thought, that he had conjured up *two* possible gay lovers and they'd ended up with each other. Life just wasn't fair.

You bitch! he thought, glaring at Quentin.

The rest of the kids at the dance thought it was bizarre. How could *two boys* be together? How would that even work? When they danced, who led? When they went on a date, who paid?

Jessica stomped over from the drink table where she'd gotten more lucky-seven punch and threw her drink in Quentin's face.

"How could you!" she cried. "You're supposed to be *my* date!"

Quentin gave her an unnerving smile as he blotted his face with a copper-colored pocket square. "Sorry, sweetie. I needed to break the spell." His eyes gleamed green.

Jessica gasped. Something about the way he called her *sweetie* seemed familiar.

Elizabeth had rushed over too, sensing her sister's distress. She took one look at Tobey and gasped, sounding exactly like her twin a few seconds earlier.

"T-Tobey?" she whispered. There was a fearful look in her aquamarine eyes.

She was remembering—and Jessica was too.

Tobey's Story

"Spell?" Jessica said hoarsely, finally taking in what her supposed date had just said. She looked from Tobey to Quentin in confusion.

Recognition now dawned in Tobey's eyes, which had become a deep sapphire blue. A smile bloomed on his ruddy lips, which sparkled from the kiss. He no longer looked like a gangly, papuliferous high school student—instead, he looked devilishly handsome.

"Thank you for waking me up from this nightmare," he said, and his words had taken on a British accent. His normal voice had returned. "... *Pepper,*" he added.

Quentin grinned, and there was something odd about his teeth. They were jagged on the bottom where they should've been straight across.

His eyes were definitely green now, not hazel.

"*Pepper?*" Jessica shrieked. "Not Pepper—*Piper!*"

"Who's Piper?" she heard someone say. A crowd had gathered around them, all keen to watch the drama unfold (especially Tom, since he must *love* drama).

"Piper," Elizabeth confirmed. "Piper Quintin."

"You're so hot," Tobey murmured, cupping Quentin's manly face in his own manly hand. His lips quirked in a smile.

"Eww, stop it," Jessica said. "I know that's not really a guy. It's a girl—a *witch*. I don't know why I didn't see it before!" She put a hand to her face in horror. Quentin had kissed her when they'd gotten out of his car! She'd been kissed by a witch in disguise!

Quentin—*Piper*—grinned slyly at her. "Saccharin Valley is *so* gender-binary. It gets boring after a while."

Both twins looked at her. Neither of them had heard the term "gender-binary". Elizabeth probably knew from computer class that "binary" meant "two"—in computer code, everything was either a one or a zero.

She wasn't sure how that applied to gender. Except that there were only two genders—right?

"Sometimes I want to wear mascara," Bruce Fatcat remarked, randomly. "It would really accentuate my already gorgeous baby blues." The other boys looked at him like he was crazy. He turned to Quentin/Piper.

161

"I'm really sorry for my behavior earlier. I think maybe I was lashing out at you because I had my own queer tendencies, deep inside."

Piper grinned.

"I like to wear masculine clothing sometimes," Lynne Henley admitted with a shrug. "The shoes are more comfortable."

"Guys' clothes *always* fit," Cara said wistfully. "Girls' sizes differ from brand to brand! It's so dumb!"

"Cara!" Lila said. "You can't be a cheerleader if you like to wear men's clothes! Besides, once you're rich enough to have your own tailor, the sizes are no longer a problem."

"Oh, of course, I'll just be rich," Cara replied sarcastically.

"I envy women's ability to create life," Ronnie Upwards spoke up. "I'm a gambling addict, but I still want to be a father. I'd be a better father than my old man was, anyway!"

"Yeah!" agreed several boys.

"I had a female roommate in college," Ms. Dalton, the French teacher and chaperone, put in. She was taking a drag on a cigarette that had appeared out of nowhere. *"C'est la vie, c'est ça l'amour."*

Jessica stamped her foot because she knew this book had lost the narrative thread. "NO!" she shouted. "Girls are girls, and boys are boys. Otherwise, it's too weird. I, for one, am *one hundred percent* woman..."

"Not *one hundred and thirty-seven* percent?" Masculine-looking Piper interjected with a sly smile, referring to a number Jessica used all the time when exaggerating, for whatever reason. (Except sometimes it was *seven* hundred and thirty-seven, and sometimes it was *three* hundred and thirty-seven. Not sure if that's from ghostwriters' lack of continuity or Jessica's supposed whimsy.)

"And you're *zero percent* man," Jessica went on hotly, regarding boyish Piper with one hand on her hip. "And that means I'm dumping you."

"Oh, sweetie, I'm way ahead of you," Piper said, giving Tobey a peck on the cheek.

Tobey's Story

"Stop doing that!" Jessica shrieked. "You still look like a boy!"

"Oh, is this better?" Before the students' very eyes, Quentin Pepper transformed, from a six-foot-tall, brawny young man to a five-foot-nine young witch. She was wearing the same suit, but it had been magically tailored to fit her witch's curves. Jessica had never seen a girl wearing mens' clothing to a dance, and somewhere in the back of her mind, she thought Piper looked really good, like a high-fashion model.

"What happened?" cried someone in the crowd.

"Quentin Pepper is a GIRL!" someone else shouted.

"Oh, then I'm *not* secretly gay?" Bruce wondered. "Phew."

"I'm a *witch,* weren't you paying attention?" Piper snarled. Her voice was no longer deep like Quentin's, but it *was* a little raspy and very menacing. She flicked a finger at Tobey, trailing sparks, and now he was no longer wearing the sorcerer's robe but a sapphire blue dress shirt with silver thorns embroidered on the collar, a black vest with silver buttons, black pants, and black ankle boots.

Of course, now *my magic works like it's supposed to,* she couldn't help thinking.

"Much better," Tobey said, looking down at his duds. "That robe was kind of itchy. They just don't know how to make quality warlock garments in Saccharin Valley."

"Too true," Piper agreed.

"If she's a witch, what's *he*?" a girl in the crowd cried in horror.

Tobey shot a dazzling smile in the girl's general direction. His lips were rosy, and his incisors were slightly pointed. "Thank you for asking, love," he said, in his suave British voice. "The term is *warlock*." He held out a hand, and a blue flame burst into existence, burning brightly without harming him.

"Ahh, there we go," he murmured. "Been trying to do that for days, seems like."

Several people gasped, and several more cowered into their cis-hetero dates.

"Oh, so you're *not* gay?" Olivia said.

"Sorry to disappoint you, ducks," he told her. "You are a lovely girl, and a talented artist, but I'm taken, I'm afraid."

"Whoever they are, neither of them belongs in Saccharin Valley!" Lila shouted in disgust. She clutched her date's arm protectively. Rowan Berry was standing there stiffly, with a dazed look in his eyes, as if he wasn't sure what was going on. Lila could tell he wasn't very brave, and any minute now he'd probably make a run for it. He was used to dealing with material wealth, not *immaterial* magic, she surmised.

"Oh, we'd better leave before they get out the torches and pitchforks," Piper said knowingly.

"Too bad," Tobey said, as he extinguished the blue flame. "Though the food left something to be desired, it *was* a pretty fab party."

"That reminds me," Piper said as she took his arm and they walked toward one of the exit doors. The crowd parted to let them go by, staring at them nervously, as if they were wild animals that had been set loose on the dance floor. Piper flicked a finger again, this time at one of the doors, and all the horseshoes over the door frames fell to the floor with loud *clanks*. A few (male) dance attendees jumped, and a few (female) ones shrieked.

"Not sure how we were permitted to enter in the first place," Tobey commented. The dance committee had been able to procure real iron horseshoes from a nearby ranch, as placing them over the doors was said to repel evil spirits.

"I'm not *evil,* I just love chaos," Piper explained as they left the gym through the exit doors. "And *you* were enchanted to already be a student here…"

Jessica ran to the door to see where they went, but they had disappeared. Which means it's back to the twins' point of view. (Yawn.)

"Good riddance," Jessica said. "Although… now I don't have a date." She looked down at her dress, which was still fabulous. It'd be a shame to not end the night in the arms of some hot guy. She peered at the crowd.

Several boys raised their hands, or jumped up and down. "Me!"

"Pick me, Jessica!"

"One dance!"

"Please!"

Jessica inspected them one by one, then shook her head and sighed. "Sorry, guys. Once you've had a gender-bending, gorgeous, supernatural date, everyone else pales in comparison."

She paused, and added, "Not that I'm *gay* or anything."

"I still have *my* gorgeous date," Lila piped up, observing Jessica's dilemma with a look of glee on her face. She turned to Rowan... and gasped.

Rowan was no longer a ruggedly handsome mortal. He was very tall and lean, with large eyes that were all black, gleaming like onyx; pointed ears, and long spindly fingers. His skin had turned a pale, sickly blue color, and an antlered crown had appeared on his head.

Large, leathery dragonfly wings unfurled from his back, ripping through the back of his suit. Once again the crowd drew back in fear.

Lila gaped up at him. "You're not human!" she cried. "What *are* you?"

He knelt before her, although kneeling down, he was still almost as tall as Lila. "I am Oberon, King of the Fey," he intoned in a deep voice. "I came to this realm seeking a bride..."

"You mean... a *queen*?" Lila's eyes widened.

He nodded, his black eyes gleaming. He took her hand in his long bony one.

"Come to the realm of Fae, my darling Lila, and rule upon high with me," he said fervently.

"You don't have to ask me twice," she said.

"What?" Jessica cried. "Lila, don't!"

A large portal opened up behind Rowan, polychromatic and sparkling, and the crowd murmured in surprise. Lila gazed at it, her brown eyes shining with wonder. She shot a triumphant look at Jessica, then picked up the hem of her long skirt and stepped through. The tall fairy creature ducked in after her, and the portal swirled closed.

Jessica's mouth dropped open. "Oh my god. She really did it."

"Lucky duck," sighed Cara.

"This dance is out of this world," added Sandra. "Witches, warlocks, fairies..."

"Did we somehow attract them with our lucky charms?" Caroline wondered. "I *told* the dance committee not to buy four-leaf clovers from that creepy plant nursery! All the plants in there looked *alive*."

Jessica scowled. "*She* gets to be a Queen of Fae? No fair." Then she shrugged, realizing if Lila was gone, that made her Number One at this dance.

The DJ started a new song, as he must've recovered from all the strange things he'd seen, remembering that he was getting paid to spin tunes at a high school dance, and not stand there gawking at various supernatural creatures.

Jessica took her sister's hand, and they began to dance together for the final song. Not like lesbians, of course. Just having fun together as sisters, and as twins.

You know, they shared that special bond, and yada yada.

"Do you think Piper and Tobey are really gone?" Elizabeth asked as she shimmied her shoulders in time with the music. (They were playing "When You Were Mine," the song that Prince wrote and Cyndi Lauper sang, without changing the genders.)

"Of course," Jessica said confidently, swaying her hips. "I mean... no, they've got to be back, because the author has a compulsion to keep writing."

"Works for me," Elizabeth said, and twirled her sister around. "We usually vanquish her in the end, anyway."

"Who, the author?"

"No, dummy, Piper."

"Oh," Jessica said. Suddenly she grabbed her wrist. "Where did my diamond tennis bracelet go?" she shrieked.

"I'm guessing it wasn't real," Elizabeth said.

Jessica pouted.

After that, Elizabeth had to go find her heteronormative (and dull-as-dishwater) date, so

Tobey's Story

Saccharin Valley would stay as it was, all sticky-sweet and flawed, instead of exploding into sparkly, witchy multi-dimensional rainbow queerness.

At least until next book...

*   *   *

Tom McLay ran outside to catch up with Tobey and Piper. A series of unbelievable things had just happened, and he needed answers, despite being a minor character.

He could see them out in the parking lot, heading towards one of the cars. "Wait!" he shouted.

The young man and the young woman turned around slowly. "Tom?" said Tobey. "What are you doing here?"

Tom eyed the red-haired woman nervously. The first boy he'd tried to conjure up was a real warlock, and the second boy was actually a girl? And not just a girl... a *witch*?

The young woman who used to be Quentin was studying him intently, and her eyes seemed to glow.

Tom's mouth opened and closed a few times. There were too many things he wanted to say. Finally, he asked, "Tobey, are you really a warlock?"

"Yes, I am," Tobey said. "As such, I don't really belong in Saccharin Valley, you must know."

Tom noticed that Tobey's voice had taken on a British accent. *He must really not be from around here,* he thought. Too bad. The warlock was really cute. He briefly imagined them settling down in a nice ruined castle somewhere, with a purebred three-headed dog, artisanal tapestries, and a tennis court in the dungeon.

"So you're not gay," he muttered. "And neither is your *girlfriend*..."

"Actually, I'm bisexual," Tobey said with a sly smile. "I was just under a spell."

"And *I'm* asexual," Piper added. "It's just that that never enters into these kinds of stories."

Tom stared at them. He didn't know what either of those words meant, since he was in Saccharin Valley in 1991.

"Well, you both can do magic, right?" he asked finally.

"Yes," Piper said with a smile. "You saw it on the dance floor." She brushed some lint off of Tobey's snazzy warlock vest.

"So why didn't either of *my* spells work?" Tom asked. There was hurt in his voice.

One of Tobey's eyebrows shot up. He looked to Piper with sudden understanding...

"Oh, is *that* how you ended up here?" Piper asked Tobey.

"It must be," Tobey said. "I was just looking over your... *scrapbook* in our world, and this bloke must've been performing his spell in Saccharin Valley at the same time."

"But how likely is it that an occult store was already in Saccharin Valley?" Piper wondered.

"It must've popped up for my character arc," Tobey said.

"A store that was run by a proprietor who was a *dead ringer* for your father back home?" Piper replied skeptically.

Tobey shrugged. "Saccharin Valley saw fit to give me a mum, and my dad had run off, so it must've borrowed my actual father's likeness for the store proprietor character."

"Hey. Guys," Tom said, snapping his fingers in their faces. "I'm still here, and I'd appreciate some answers." At the same time, he was thinking, *"our world"?* Were these two magical teenagers some sort of inter-dimensional travelers?

Tobey turned back to Tom. "Well, I suppose both your spells *did* work... just not in the way you intended," he said apologetically. "I'm sorry, mate."

"Saccharin Valley tends to be resistant to magic," Piper put it. "I find it easier to navigate when I come here of my own accord... *and* when I'm dealing solely with Jessica and Elizabeth Wastefeld."

Tom's brow furrowed. "Jessica and Elizabeth? Why them?"

"They're the main characters," Piper said with a shrug.

Tobey's Story

Tom somehow knew exactly what she meant. At the same time, he felt like there was a whole world of information that these two weren't letting on, and he wanted to know *everything*. Realizing he was gay was one thing, but learning that magic was real...

"I think I know why a portal hasn't opened up yet, for us to make our exit," Tobey said to Piper, his sapphire eyes shining. "We need to do a good deed before we go."

"Oh, that'll be a lovely ending," Piper agreed. "I always wanted to be a fairy godmother... to someone other than the spoiled-brat Wastefeld twins, of course."

Tom's eyes widened. "What's happening?"

But he was interrupted by them starting to chant in tandem. He couldn't make out the words, as they seemed to be in Latin. Tobey's eyes were glowing blue, and Piper's eyes were glowing green. Tobey held up his left hand, and Piper held up her right. Purple magic pulsated from her hands, and blue from his, combining into a cloud of deep indigo energy.

Before Tom could say anything else, there was a bright flash of light that dazzled his eyes. He shut them tightly, and when he opened them and the spots cleared, the two young magic practitioners were gone.

Tom stared at the space where they'd been in astonishment.

Then he slowly turned and started walking back into the school. *That was too weird.*

Before he got to the door, a car pulled up.

"Need a ride?" called a hunky voice.

Tom looked up. It was Jake Flairell, Enid's cousin—the only other gay around these parts, and therefore his soulmate.

He broke into a grin.

"Absolutely."

*   *   *

When the dance was winding down and Jessica and Elizabeth were walking out to meet Todd's car, a portal opened up in front of them, and Lila was spat out of it, covered in some sort of iridescent ooze.

"That was disgusting," she sputtered as she staggered to her feet. "All those *creatures*. Some had wings, some had horns, some had antennae!" She shuddered. "Why would I want to be a queen of another world when I'm already a princess here in Saccharin Valley?"

"Aww, I missed you, Li," Jessica said with a smile.

"Why don't you ride home with us and tell us all about it?" Elizabeth added.

Epilogue

Saturday morning, Jake drove Tom downtown. "Tell me more about this occult store," he said, popping a jazz tape into the cassette player.

"I don't know much," Tom said with a shrug. "It just sort of appeared one day."

"But *that's* how you got me back into your life? With a spell from an old book?" Jake's eyes glittered with mischief. He didn't know whether Tom had been teasing when he'd told him that. But it didn't matter much, since it was close to the end of the book, and they were together again. "I thought you were into sci-fi, not fantasy."

The store was empty when they pulled up. "This isn't it," Tom explained as they got out of the car. "It's in the... basement?"

He stopped abruptly in the entrance to the alley. There was no sign... and no stairs. Just concrete with patches of grass growing in the cracks.

"A basement? In California?" Jake looked at Tom with incredulity.

"It was right here," Tom protested. "Where did it go?"

Jake gave him a kiss on the cheek, which was probably all that was permitted in these books. "Come on, hon. The store is gone, but I'm still here. Let's get tacos."

Tom rubbed his eyes, then followed his new boyfriend back to the car.

ABOUT THE AUTHOR

Polly Esther Rayon is a Millennial, childfree singleton who uses reading, writing, drawing and other creative pursuits to cope with her various medical conditions, including hydrocephalus, chronic pain and depression. She has been obsessed with Sweet Valley since the 4th grade, although that turned into a love-hate relationship as a teenager. When not writing like a maniac, she likes to make art, play guitar and befriend everyone's cats.

Follow Polly Esther Rayon on:
Facebook/saccharinvalleytwits
Instagram & TikTok @pollyestherrayon

saccharinvalleytwits.blogspot.com

COULD *YOU* BE THE NEXT SACCHARIN VALLEY HEXED READER OF THE MONTH?

**Calling all Saccharin Valley Fiends!
Here's a chance to be cursed for all eternity, with your visage haunting the back of a
Saccharin Valley book!**

We know how important Saccharin Valley is to you... our familiar told us in the dead of night. We know you would sacrifice your firstborn child to the Powers of Darkness for another Saccharin Valley book. That's why we've come up with a macabre celebration offering terrifying opportunities to have your image and thoughts imprisoned in a Saccharin Valley tome.

"How do I become one of the Accursed?"

It's easy. Simply write an essay in your own blood (100 words or less, we don't want you to faint), telling us how you best worship chaos by reading these hideous tales, whether at midnight under a dark moon, or deep in a forest blanketed in sinister mist, where owls screech and spirits haunt the dead, blackened branches of trees. Place your essay betwixt the beak of your local raven, or bury it in a fresh grave and let the earthworms convey it to us.

We (the Unseen Servants of Darkness) will pick the best essays and print them, along with the Damned's infernal portrait, in the back of an upcoming book (you will be able to stay young while your portrait withers and ages, so long as you keep reading these ghastly books).

And there's more!

One damned soul will win a one-way trip to your local Fiendish Pit, where a perpetual party rages on and on, with your favorite witches, demons, and vampires in attendance.

(P. S. I just noticed the address in the back of SVH books was *666* Fifth Avenue, how apropos).

Made in the USA
Coppell, TX
05 February 2026